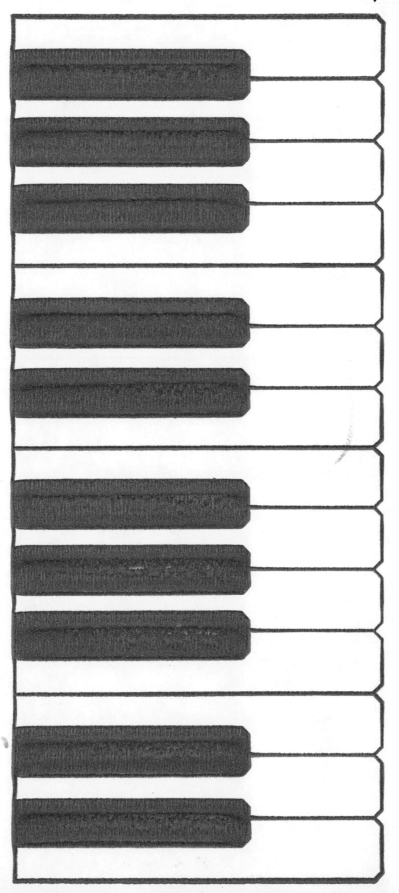

SILVER BURDETT music

ELIZABETH CROOK
BENNETT REIMER
DAVID S. WALKER

SILVER BURDETT COMPANY

MORRISTOWN, NEW JERSEY · GLENVIEW, ILLINOIS
PALO ALTO · DALLAS · ATLANTA

SPECIAL CONTRIBUTORS

William M. Anderson (non-Western music), Aurora, Ohio

Kojo Fosu Baiden (music of Africa), Silver Springs, Maryland

Dulce B. Bohn (recorder), Wilmington, Delaware

Charles L. Boilès (music of Mexico), Bloomington, Indiana

Ian L. Bradley (Canadian music), Victoria, British Columbia, Canada

Gerald Burakoff (recorder), Levittown, New York

Henry Burnett (music of Japan), Flushing, Long Island, New York

Richard J. Colwell (testing and evaluation), Urbana, Illinois

Marilyn C. Davidson (music for Orff instruments), Bergenfield, New Jersey

Joan Davies (music of Canada and Japan), Charlottetown, P.E.I., Canada

Kay Hardesty (special education), Chautauqua, New York

James M. Harris (music in early childhood), San Francisco, California

Doris E. Hays (avant-garde music), New York City

Nazir A. Jairazbhoy (music of India), Windsor, Ontario, Canada

Maria Jordan (music of Greece), Hicksville, Long Island, New York

Robert A. Kauffman (music of Africa), Seattle, Washington

Edna Knock (music of Canada), Brandon, Manitoba, Canada

John Lidstone (visual arts), Brooklyn, New York

David McHugh (youth music), New York City

Alan P. Merriam (music of the North American Indians), Bloomington, Indiana

Lucille Mitchell (American folk songs), Alexandria, Virginia

Maria Luisa Muñoz (music of Puerto Rico), Houston, Texas

Lynn Freeman Olson (listening program), New York City

Mary E. Perrin (music in the inner city), Chicago, Illinois

Carmino Ravosa (children's song literature), Briarcliff Manor, New York

Joyce Bogusky-Reimer (avant-garde music), Wilmette, Illinois

Geraldine Slaughter (music of Africa), Washington, D.C.

Mark Slobin (music of the Near East), Middletown, Connecticut

Ruth Marie Stone (music of Africa), New York City

Leona B. Wilkins (music in the inner city), Evanston, Illinois

CONSULTANTS

Lynn Arizzi (levels 1 and 2), Reston, Virginia

Joy Browne (levels 5 and 6), Kansas City, Missouri

Nancy Crump, classroom teacher, Alexandria, Louisiana

Lyla Evans, classroom teacher, South Euclid, Ohio

Catherine Gallas, classroom teacher, Bridgeton, Missouri

Linda Haselton, classroom teacher, Westminster, California

Ruth A. Held, classroom teacher, Lancaster, Pennsylvania

Judy F. Jackson, classroom teacher, Franklin, Tennessee

Mary E. Justice, Auburn University, Auburn, Alabama

Jean Lembke (levels 3 and 4), Tonawanda, New York

Barbara Nelson, classroom teacher, Baytown, Texas

Terry Philips (youth music), New York City

Ruth Red, Director of Music Education, Houston, Texas

Mary Ann Shealy (levels 1 and 2), Florence, South Carolina

Beatrice Schattschneider (levels 1–6), Morristown, New Jersey

Paulette Schmalz, classroom teacher, Phoenix, Arizona

Sister Helen C. Schneider, Clarke College, Dubuque, Iowa

Merrill Staton (recordings), Alpine, New Jersey

ACKNOWLEDGMENTS

The authors and editors of SILVER BURDETT MUSIC acknowledge with gratitude the contributions of the following persons.

Marjorie Hahn, New York
Yoriko Kozumi, Japan
Ruth Merrill, Texas
Mary Ann Nelson, Texas
Bennie Mae Oliver, Texas
Joanne Ryan, New York
Helen Spiers, Virginia
Shirley Ventrone, Rhode Island
Avonelle Walker, New York

Credit and appreciation are due publishers and copyright owners for use of the following.

"April Rain Song" from THE DREAM KEEPER, by Langston Hughes. Copyright 1932 and renewed 1960 by Langston Hughes. Reprinted by permission of Alfred A. Knopf, Inc.

"At the Top of My Voice" from AT THE TOP OF MY VOICE AND OTHER POEMS, by Felice Holman, is reprinted by permission of Charles Scribner's Sons. Copyright © 1970 by Felice Holman.

"Chanticleer"—Reprinted by permission of Yale University Press from SONGS FOR PARENTS, by John Farrar. Copyright © 1921 by Yale University Press.

"The House Cat" from the book FOR DAYS AND DAYS by Annette Wynne. Copyright, 1919, by J. B. Lippincott Company. Renewal, 1947, by Annette Wynne. Reprinted by permission of J. B. Lippincott Company.

"I Like Winter, Spring, Summer, and Fall" from A BUNCH OF POEMS AND VERSES by Beatrice Schenk de Regniers, A Clarion Book. Reprinted by permission of Houghton Mifflin/Clarion Books.

"Lazy Jane" text and art, from WHERE THE SIDEWALK ENDS: The Poems and Drawings of Shel Silverstein. Copyright © 1974 by Shel Silverstein. Reprinted by permission of Harper and Row, Publishers, Inc.

"The Leaves Turn Gold" from A BUNCH OF POEMS AND VERSES by Beatrice Schenk de Regniers, A Clarion Book. Used by permission of Houghton Mifflin/Clarion Books.

"On Halloween" by Shel Silverstein. Copyright © 1963 by Shel Silverstein. From POEMS FOR SEASONS AND CELEBRATIONS by William Cole.

"Summer Song" from THE MAN WHO SANG THE SILLIES by John Ciardi. Copyright © 1961 by John Ciardi. Reprinted by permission of J. B. Lippincott, Publishers.

"The White Window" from COLLECTED POEMS by James Stephens. Copyright 1915 by Macmillan Publishing Co., Inc., renewed 1943 by James Stephens. Reprinted by permission of Macmillan Publishing Co., Inc., Mrs. Iris Wise and Macmillan, London and Basingstoke.

CONTENTS

THINGS YOU CAN DO WITH MUSIC

SING

MORE THINGS YOU CAN DO WITH MUSIC

PLAY

LISTEN

FAST—SLOW

People and things move *fast* and *slow*.

How would it feel to be a car going *fast*?

How would it feel to be a car going *slow*?

What things move SLOW?

What things move FAST?

7

HIGH—LOW

$\uparrow$

HIGH

LOW

$\downarrow$

Some music is HIGH.
Some music is LOW.

Listen to "The Critter Got Away."

Does the music end *high* or *low?*

How does the music begin?

Find the arrow that shows how the song begins.

Find the arrow that shows how the song ends.

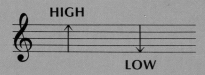

Which notes are high on the staff?

Which notes are low on the staff?

Play one note after the other on the bells.

Play all through the song.

Read from left to right.

Play high and low on these instruments, or on instruments like them.

Alto metallophone

Soprano xylophone

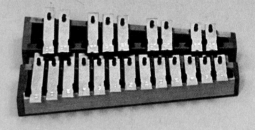

Soprano glockenspiel

Alto xylophone

Where are the higher sounds?

Where are the lower sounds?

Find high C.

Find low C.

Play high C and low C as you sing.

Read from left to right.

THE ARTS: DIRECTION AND LINE

Can you find curved lines in these pictures?

Can you find straight lines?

STEADY BEAT—NO BEAT

Can you tell what is happening in each picture?

Listen to these sounds.

Which sound goes with which picture?

Which sounds have a *steady beat*?

You can say poems with a steady beat.

You can say poems with no beat.

How will you say these poems?

THE LEAVES TURN GOLD

The leaves turn gold
                    in the fall.
Turn red, turn old
                    in the fall.
Fall down, turn brown,
Grumble
And crumble
Under my feet
                    in the fall.

Beatrice Schenk de Regniers

AT THE TOP OF MY VOICE

When I stamp

The ground thunders,

When I shout

The world rings,

When I sing

The air wonders

How I do such things.

Felice Holman

Some music has a steady beat.

Some music has no beat.

Follow the lines as you hear steady beats.

What does this drawing show?

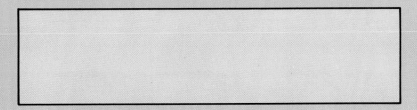

Steady beats may be written as quarter notes.

On the staff, the quarter notes show the note G.

G

Play G on the bells as others sing *Mama Paquita*.

WHOA, MULE   BLACK-AMERICAN FOLK SONG

Play G F♯ E D on bells, as others sing Section B of "Whoa, Mule."

What tells you to play steady beats?

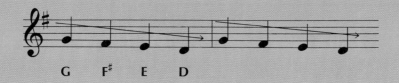

G   F♯   E   D

A   Whoa, mule, whoa, mule,

Whoa, mule, I tell you,

Whoa, mule, I say!

Tied a slip-knot in his tail

And his head slipped through the collar.

Hurry, hurry, save us,

Hee-haw, hee-haw, hee-haw!

Hurry, hurry, save us!

Whoa, mule, I say!

B   Whoa, mule, I tell you,

Whoa, mule, I say!

Ain't got time to kiss you now,

But don't you run away.

SOUND PIECE 1: Bodybeat

JOYCE BOGUSKY-REIMER

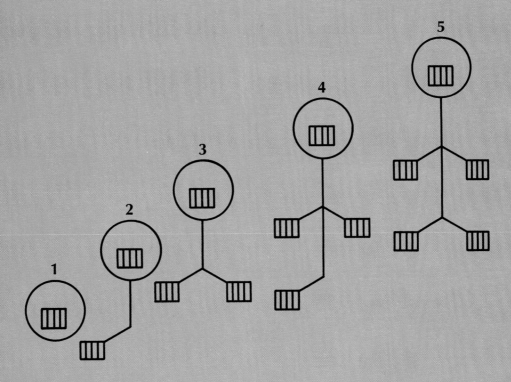

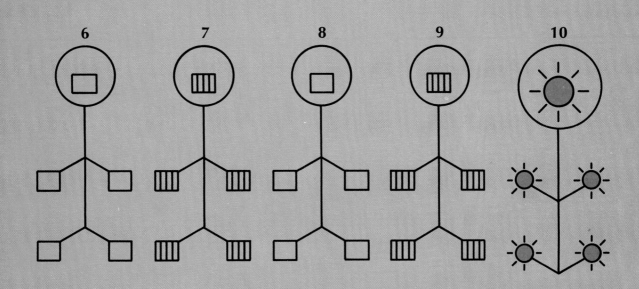

UPWARD—DOWNWARD

Which way do the lines swoop
in this drawing?

How many swoops do you see?

Make your voice swoop upward
as many times as the drawing shows.

Now follow the lines
that swoop downward.

Make your voice do
what the lines on this staff show.

SOUND PIECE 2: Swoop It Up and Down

The lines on the staff move upward and downward.
Play bells upward and downward just like the lines.

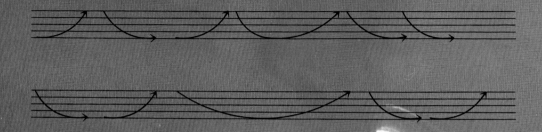

Someone else can move with a flashlight upward and downward.
Follow the lines on the staff.

Can you see lines that show movement downward?

Can you see lines that show movement upward?

Can you see lines that show movement upward and downward?

Can you see notes that move upward?

Can you see notes that move downward?

Can you see notes that move upward and downward?

1

D D E F♯ G
Don't you run a - way.

2

A A G G F
Do re - mem - ber me.

3

D E F♯ E D
Hal - le - lu - jah

SWEETHEART OUT A-HUNTING

PLAY PARTY SONG FROM TENNESSEE

1. Sweetheart out a-hunting on a long *summer day*,
   Sweetheart out a-hunting on a long *summer day*.
   Swing Eliza, swing her, on a long *summer day*,
   Swing Eliza, swing her, on a long *summer day*.

2. Where will he find her on a long *summer day*?
   Where will he find her on a long *summer day*?
   Swing Eliza, swing her, on a long *summer day*,
   Swing Eliza, swing her, on a long *summer day*.

3. Go up head and find her on a long *summer day*,
   Go up head and find her on a long *summer day*.
   Swing, Eliza, swing her, on a long *summer day*,
   Swing, Eliza, swing her, on a long *summer day*.

4. Walk and talk together on a long *summer day*,
   Walk and talk together on a long *summer day*.
   Swing, Eliza, swing her, on a long *summer day*,
   Swing, Eliza, swing her, on a long *summer day*.

SUO GAN

WELSH FOLK MELODY   ENGLISH WORDS BY DAVID S. WALKER

1. Su - o gan, in the west,

Su - o gan, sun has set,

Su - o gan, ver - y soon,

Su - o gan, shines the moon.

2. Suo gan, now the stars,

Suo gan, shine from far,

Suo gan, giving light,

Suo gan, through the night.

3. Suo gan, then at dawn,

Suo gan, in the morn,

Suo gan, sun appears,

Suo gan, day is here.

Find the notes that move in an upward direction.

Find the notes that move in a downward direction.

LADY, COME FOLK SONG FROM ENGLAND

La - dy, come, Can't you see?

John fell off the white oak tree.

Find bells G, A, and B.

Play the notes in the color blocks.

Find this pattern in the song.

F   E   D   C

How many times do you see it?

Does it move upward, or downward?

MY SILVER WHISTLE
SLOVENIAN FOLK TUNE   ENGLISH WORDS BY MARTHA GIBSON

Lis - ten to the blar - ing of my sil - ver whis - tle!

Lis - ten to the blar - ing of my sil - ver whis - tle!

Blow, blow, what a blast! Shat - ter chi - na, shat - ter glass!

Oh, ho! What a life! When you've got a whis - tle.

LOUD—
SOFT

Which pictures show things that make soft sounds?

Which pictures show things that make loud sounds?

CHANTICLEER

High and proud on the barnyard fence
Walks rooster in the morning.
He shakes his comb, he shakes his tail
And gives his daily warning.
"Get up, you lazy boys and girls,
It's time you should be dressing!"
I wonder if he keeps a clock,
Or if he's only guessing.

John Farrar

Follow the words as you listen to these poems.

Which poem is mostly *loud?*

Which poem is mostly *soft?*

APRIL RAIN SONG

Let the rain kiss you.

Let the rain beat upon your head with silver liquid drops.

Let the rain sing you a lullaby.

The rain makes still pools on the sidewalk.

The rain makes running pools in the gutter.

The rain plays a little sleep-song on our roof at night—

And I love the rain.

Langston Hughes

THE BAND IN THE SQUARE

WORDS AND MUSIC BY CARMINO RAVOSA

Play four times

(A) Here comes the band,

Way down the street.

You can hear the music;

You can hear the beat.

There's music in the air,

You can feel it everywhere;

It's the band, it's the band in the square.

Soft to Loud

(Listen to the band.)

Play four times   **Loud**

(A) There goes the band,

Off down the street.

You can hear the music;

You can hear the beat.

There's music in the air,

You can feel it everywhere;

It's the band, it's the band in the square.

Loud to Soft

FLOWERS WON'T GROW

MUSIC BY JIM HUNTER   WORDS BY TOM PAISLEY

Flowers won't grow

If we throw junk on the ground

And stuff all around.

The flowers won't grow,

The flowers won't grow.

Birds go away,

They won't play where there's junk on the ground

And stuff all around.

The birds go away,

The birds go away.

If the flowers won't grow

And the birds go away,

Well, where would we go to have fun and play?

Now that you know,

I bet you won't throw

Junk on the ground

And stuff all around

So the birds will play

And   flowers will grow,

flowers will grow,

flowers will grow,

flowers will grow.

E   D

Play softer

softer

softer

Each clock has a special look, or *style*.
How are they different?

FORM

Shake Hands, Mary has two sections.

The sections are different.

How do these shapes show the different sections?

Play as others sing the first section.

Play as others sing the second section.

In music, letters can show different sections.

The form of *Shake Hands, Mary* is AB.

HURRY, LITTLE PONY

FOLK SONG FROM SPAIN   ARRANGED BY BRIAN BONSOR

ENGLISH WORDS BY ELIZABETH BARNARD

FROM CHILDREN'S SONGS FROM SPAIN. COPYRIGHT © 1957 J. CURWEN AND SONS, LTD. USED BY PERMISSION.

Can you sound like the pony's hooves?

Use your mouth to make the sound.

INTRODUCTION

clicks

1. Hur - ry, lit - tle po - ny, Gal - lop on the way,
2. Hur - ry, lit - tle po - ny, To the sta - ble go,
3. Hur - ry, lit - tle po - ny, We must find the Child,

For we must be ear - ly, Don't be late to - day.
We shall find a ba - by, In a man - ger low.
Born of Moth - er Ma - ry, Je - sus, meek and mild.

B Hurry, hurry, hurry or we shan't be early,

Hurry, hurry, hurry or we shan't be early,

Hurry, hurry, hurry or we shan't be early,

Hurry, little pony, on the way.

ENDING

Hurry, little pony, hurry, little pony,

 on the way.

clicks

37

Get On Board has a different form.

What do these shapes show about the form?

A Maracas

B Sandblocks

A Maracas

SHOO FLY
AMERICAN GAME SONG

How will you play the tambourine when A comes back?

How will you play the drum when A comes back?

Play the bells in Section A or Section B.

High C

Low C

39

BEST FRIENDS

WORDS BY MARGARET JONES

© 1971 CARMINO RAVOSA AND MARGARET JONES

Refrain

A

Best friends should be together,

That's how it ought to be,

So let's pretend I'm part of you

and you are part of me.

Verse 1

B

If you were a little shoe,

I would be your heel;

If you were a little pig,

I would be your squeal.

If you were a little peach,

I could be your fuzz;

If you were a bumblebee,

I could be your buzz.

Refrain

A

Best friends should be together,

That's how it ought to be,

So let's pretend I'm part of you

and you are part of me.

Verse 2

If you were an elephant,

I could be your trunk;

If you were a choc'late cake,

I would be a hunk.

If you were a picture,

I could be your frame;

But if you were nothing,

I'd like you just the same. *Refrain*

Which shapes and letters show the form of "Best Friends?"

A   B

A   B   A

Show the ABA form as you perform the song.

A   **ALL SING**   Clap hands to the steady beat.

B   **SING A SOLO**

A   **ALL SING**   Clap hands to the steady beat.

THE ARTS: ACTIVE—STILL

Which of these paintings feels more active?

Which feels more still?

METER

BEATS GROUPED IN TWOS

Feel the sets of 2 as you say this chant.

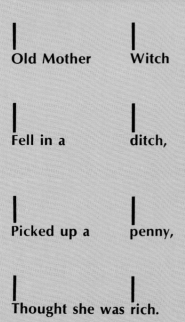

Old Mother	Witch
Fell in a	ditch,
Picked up a	penny,
Thought she was	rich.

In music, *quarter notes* can show beats.

Follow the *quarter notes* in sets of 2 as you say the chant.

BEATS GROUPED IN THREES

Feel the sets of 3 as you say this chant.

| Old Mother	| Witch
| Fell in a	| ditch,
| Picked up a	| penny,
| Thought she was	| rich.

In music, quarter notes can show beats.

Follow the quarter notes in sets of 3 as you say the chant.

Choose your own instrument to play on the third beat of each set.

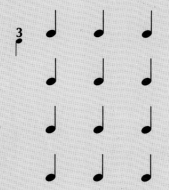

THE CRITTER GOT AWAY

FOLK TUNE FROM POLAND

ENGLISH WORDS BY MARGARET MARKS

1. "Who's been eating up my corn?"
   Cried the farmer one fine morn;
   Saw a rabbit, tried to grab it,
   But the critter got away!

2. "Who's been eating up my squash?"
   Cried the farmer, "Well, by gosh!"
   Saw a groundhog, called his hound dog,
   But the critter got away!

3. "Who's been eating up my peas?"
   Cried the farmer, "If you please!"
   Saw a chipmunk and a big skunk,
   But the critters got away!

4. "Who's been eating up my rye?"
   Cried the farmer, "Me oh my!"
   Saw a possum, did he cuss him!
   But the critter got away!

5. Cried the farmer, "What's the use?
   Critters eat what I produce!
   Chipmunk, rabbit, I have had it!"
   And the farmer went away!

Follow the quarter notes in sets of 2 as you play.

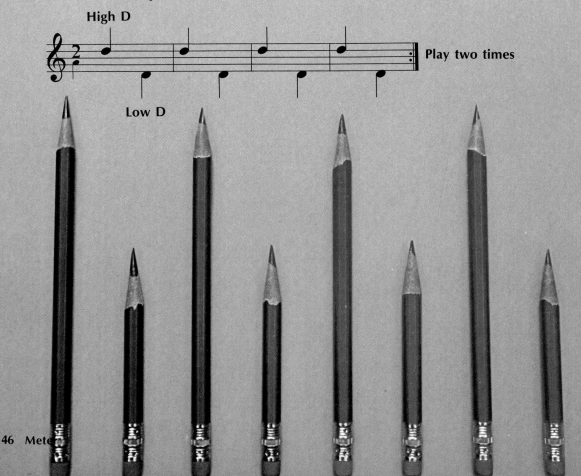

High D

Low D

Play two times

THE VILLAGE DANCE YIDDISH FOLK SONG

ENGLISH WORDS BY ROSEMARY JACQUES

1. Each evening in the village
   People gather round,
   People gather round;
   Each evening in the village
   People gather round the square.

2. Girls wearing pretty dresses
   Circle round and round,
   Circle round and round;
   Girls wearing pretty dresses
   Circle round and round the square.

3. Young men in brilliant colors
   Whirl their partners round,
   Whirl their partners round;
   Young men in brilliant colors
   Whirl their partners round the square.

4. Everyone sings and dances
   When they gather round,
   When they gather round;
   Everyone sings and dances
   When they gather round the square.

Follow the quarter notes in sets of 3 as you play.

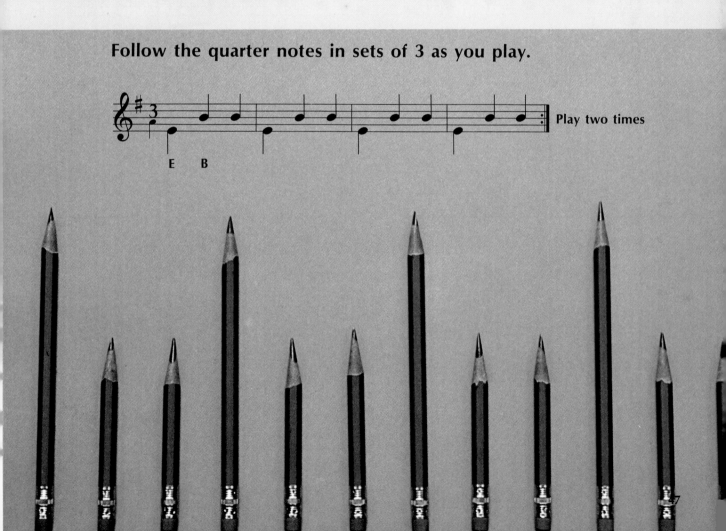

E   B

Play two times

METER IN TWO

THE FROG SONG TRADITIONAL

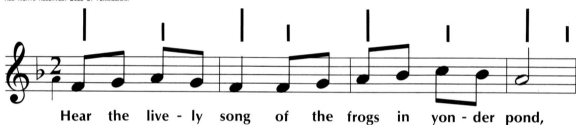

Hear the live - ly song of the frogs in yon - der pond,

Krik, krik, krik, krik, krik, krik, Brrr - um!

Show sets of two beats by strumming Autoharp strings.

Someone will help you by pressing the chord button F.

Play sets of two beats on the bells.

METER IN THREE

SOMMER, ADE! FOLK SONG FROM GERMANY ENGLISH WORDS BY ALICE FIRGAU

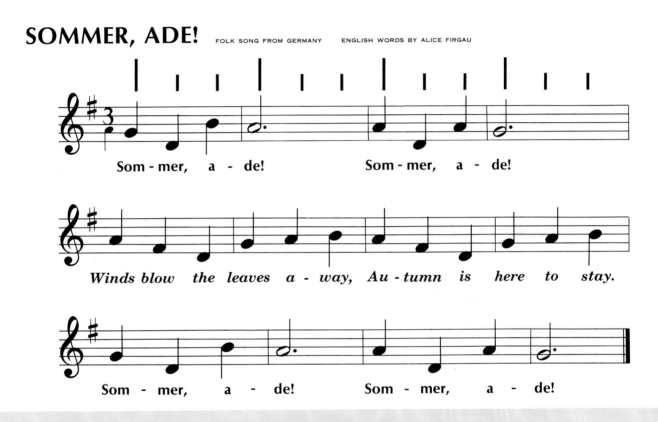

Som - mer, a - de! Som - mer, a - de!

Winds blow the leaves a - way, Au - tumn is here to stay.

Som - mer, a - de! Som - mer, a - de!

Show sets of three beats by strumming Autoharp strings.

Someone will help you by pressing chord buttons G and D₇.

Play sets of three beats on the bells to the words *Sommer, ade.*

FAST—SLOW

A fast TEMPO feels right for some music.

A slow TEMPO is better for other music.

Guess what TEMPO to expect in this song.

CRADLE HYMN FOLK SONG FROM KENTUCKY

FROM DEVIL'S DITTIES BY JEAN THOMAS, P. 79. COPYRIGHT 1931 BY WILBUR HATFIELD. REPRINTED BY PERMISSION OF JEAN THOMAS, THE TRAIPSIN' WOMAN.

Hush, my babe, lie still and slum - ber; Ho - ly an-gels guard your bed.

Heav'n-ly bless - ings with-out num - ber gent - ly steal-ing on your head.

What tempo do you expect in this song?

Here are some of the words.

OLD MOLLY HARE AMERICAN FOLK SONG

1. Old Mol - ly Hare,_____

What you do - ing there?_____

Run - ning through the cot - ton just as fast as I can tear.

2. Old Molly Hare,

   What you doing there?

   Eating up the apples and a-looking for a pear.

3. Nibbling in the garden just as often as I dare.

4. Picking out a briar, sitting on a prickly pear.

5. Sitting on a haystack and a-shooting at a bear.

Which drawing shows the steady beat?

Which drawing shows beats getting faster?

Which drawing shows beats getting slower?

1.   2.   3.

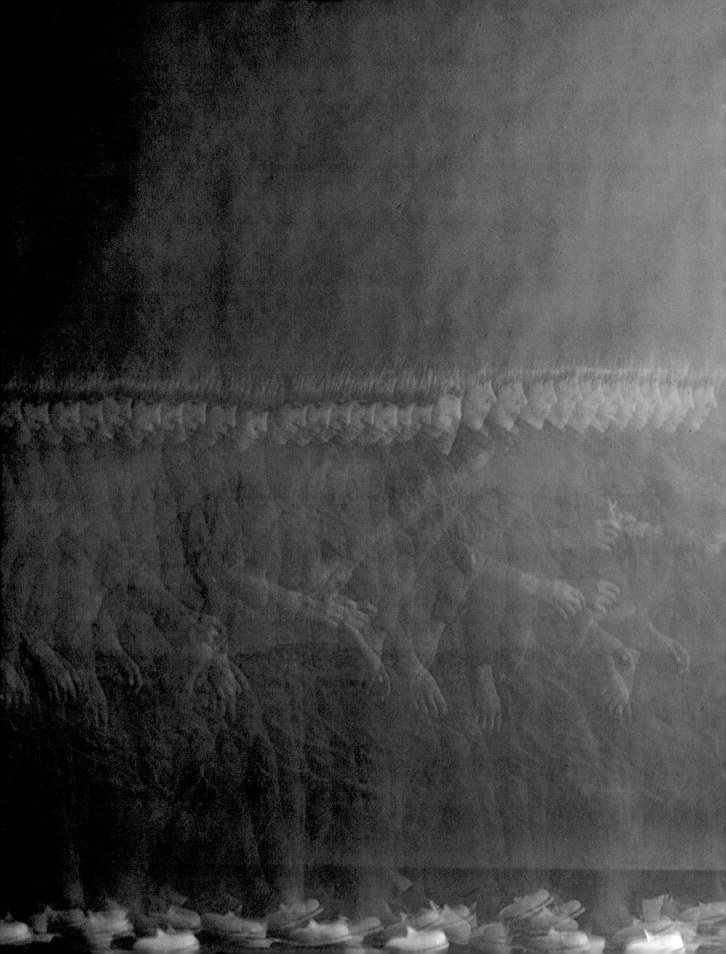

ACCENT—NO ACCENT

Listen for the accents (>) in this song.

Play the accents. The music shows what bells to play.

THE LITTLE QUAILS   FOLK SONG FROM POLAND   ENGLISH WORDS BY KAROL GULBISH

1. Once a happy little quail sang, "Bobwhite,"

D

Such a pretty little quail sang, "Bobwhite,"

C

As she ran and played along the tall grass,

B♭

As she stood and watched the fluffy clouds pass.

F

2. Came along a handsome quail named Bob White,

"Tell me that you'll be my bride," sang Bob White;

She replied, "Sir, you must ask my mother,

And my father and my little brother."

3. Both his wings were shaky as they could be

When he went to see his sweetheart's fam'ly,

But he had no reason to be nervous,

For her parents and her brother said, "Yes."

4. Now a handsome, happy quail named Bob White

And his very pretty Missus Bob White

Love to run and play among the tall grass,

Love to stand and watch the fluffy clouds pass.

Now play accents on other instruments.

 on a drum,

 a tambourine,

 or a wood block.

Find the *accented* quarter notes.

Choose one line to play

1.

2.

3.

4.

Why does each line of quarter notes

sound different?

Can someone tell which line

you played?

STYLE: AFRICAN MUSIC

Music is used by people around the world.

People sing music.

People play musical instruments.

People dance, or move to music.

People compose music.

People listen to music.

What do you hear in this music of Africa?

Listen to the Call Chart.

The numbers tell you what to hear.

CALL CHART
1. *MANY MEN SINGING*
2. *STEADY BEAT*
3. *ACCENTS*
4. *MANY DIFFERENT RHYTHMS*

LONG—SHORT

Which pictures show children taking long steps?

Which pictures show children taking short steps?

Which lines show long steps?

Which lines show short steps?

On which instrument can you play long sounds?

On which instrument can you play short sounds?

Which instrument plays both long and short sounds?

finger cymbals

Choose an instrument.

Make up your own music.

Play both long and short sounds.

Will you play alone, or with a partner?

Will you play loud, or soft?

Will you play many accents, or few accents?

autoharp

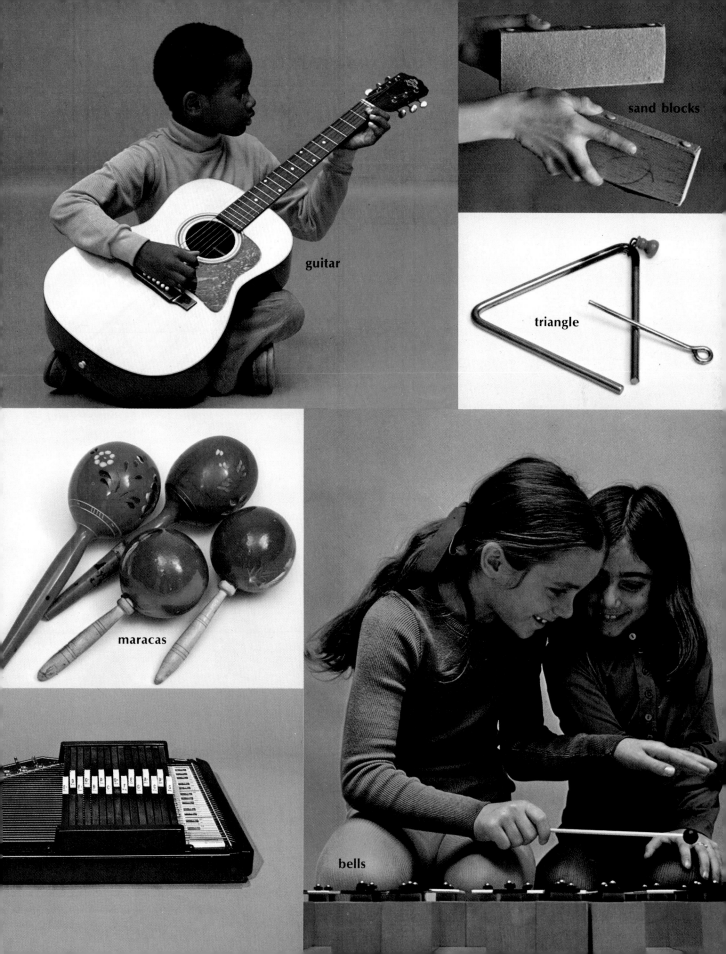

guitar

sand blocks

triangle

maracas

bells

A bell plays long sounds.

Maracas play short sounds.

Choose one to play.

LULLA, LULLABY   FOLK SONG FROM MEXICO   ENGLISH VERSION BY VERNE MUÑOZ

Hush, my lit - tle ba - by,

Close your sleep - y eyes;____

I will sing a song for you,

Lul - la, lul - la - by.____

Look at the words in the title.

Will you hear long sounds or short sounds?

HOP UP AND JUMP UP SHAKER HYMN

FROM THE GIFT TO BE SIMPLE BY EDWARD DEMING ANDREWS. COPYRIGHT © 1940 BY EDWARD D. ANDREWS.

Hop up and jump up and whirl round, whirl round,

Gath - er love, here it is all round, all round.

Here is love flow - ing round, catch it as you whirl round,

Reach up and reach down, here it is all round.

The short notes ♪♪ are called *eighth notes*.

Play this part on a wood block as others sing.

Play eight times

63

RINGING BELLS

FOLK SONG FROM GERMANY   ENGLISH VERSION BY TRUDI EICHENLAUB

FROM SING MIT. SONGBOOK FOR LOWER GRADES OF PUBLIC SCHOOLS. PUBLISHER: R. OLDENBOURG. MUNICH 1964. REPRINTED BY PERMISSION.

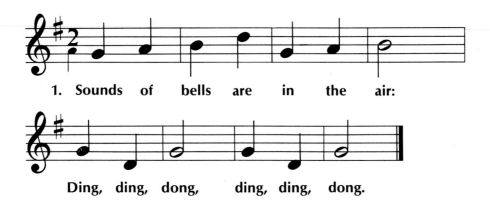

1. Sounds of bells are in the air:

Ding, ding, dong, ding, ding, dong.

2. Time to wake up, morning's here:

Ding, ding, dong, ding, ding, dong.

Play the steady beat on bells while others sing.

Hold a mallet in each hand.

quarter notes

G   D

Now play long sounds while others sing.

half notes

G

How is the long sound written?

This note is called a *half note*.

Play rhythm sticks as you sing each word.

Are there mostly long sounds, or short sounds?

HOLD MY MULE BLACK-AMERICAN FOLK SONG

FROM ON THE TRAIL OF NEGRO FOLK-SONGS BY DOROTHY SCARBOROUGH. COPYRIGHT, 1925, BY HARVARD UNIVERSITY PRESS; 1953 BY MARY MCDANIEL PARKER. REPRINTED BY PERMISSION.

1. Hold my mule while I dance Jo - sey,

Hold my mule while I dance Jo - sey,

Hold my mule while I dance Jo - sey,

Oh, Miss Su - san Brown.

2. Wouldn't give a nickel if I couldn't dance Josey, (*3 times*)
   Oh, Miss Susan Brown.

3. Had a glass of buttermilk and I danced Josey, (*3 times*)
   Oh, Miss Susan Brown.

Play this part on a triangle.

 Repeat

Notes can show long and short sounds.

Which notes show the longest sound?
Which notes show the shortest sound?

The half note shows the long sound.

The quarter note shows a shorter sound.

The *eighth notes* show the shortest sounds.

These patterns use both long and short sounds.

Play them on a percussion instrument.

Check your playing with the recording.

USING WHAT YOU KNOW ABOUT MUSIC

ON THE SEASONS

I like winter, spring, summer, and fall.

In the fall I like fall best of all.

What I like most is

A witch or a ghost is

Quite likely to pay me a call.

Beatrice Schenk de Regniers

ON HALLOWEEN

On Halloween I'll go to town

And wear my trousers upside down,

And wear my shoes turned inside out

And wear a wig of sauerkraut.

Shel Silverstein

THE GHOST OF JOHN
WORDS AND MUSIC BY MARTHA GRUBB

Have you seen the ghost of John?

Long white bones and his skin all gone,_____

Oo,   oo,_____

Would-n't it be chil-ly with no skin on!

THANKSGIVING
FOLK SONG FROM FINLAND   ENGLISH WORDS BY ROSEMARY JACQUES

1. For the sun that gives us light,   *We are truly thankful.*
   For the moon that shines at night,   *We are truly thankful.*
   For the twinkling stars so bright,   *We are truly thankful.*

2. For the corn and golden wheat,   *We are truly thankful.*
   For the pears and apples sweet,   *We are truly thankful.*
   For the good food that we eat,   *We are truly thankful.*

3. For the joys of each new day,   *We are truly thankful.*
   For each hour of work and play,   *We are truly thankful.*
   For God's blessings, let us say,   *"We are truly thankful."*

Play one of the parts as others sing *We are truly thankful.*

Find the color block.

Do the notes move upward or downward?

AMERICA
TRADITIONAL   WORDS BY SAMUEL FRANCIS SMITH

My coun - try! 'tis   of thee, Sweet land of   lib - er - ty,

Of   thee   I   sing;

Land where my   fa - thers died, Land   of   the   Pil - grims' pride,

From ev - 'ry____ moun - tain - side

Let____ free - dom   ring!

Our fathers' God, to Thee,

Author of liberty,

To Thee we sing;

Long may our land be bright

With Freedom's holy light;

Protect us by Thy might,

Great God, our King!

Play the note in the color block.

Will you play the same note each time?

AY, DI, DI, DI

HASIDIC MELODY

Ay, di, di, di, ay, di, di, di, di;

Ay, di, di, di, di, ay, di, di, di, di.

Ay, di, di, di, ay, di, di, di, di;

Ay, di, di, di, di, ay, di, di, di, di.

Listen to the recording of *Halloween*, by Charles Ives.

Find the word or symbol in each box that shows what you hear.

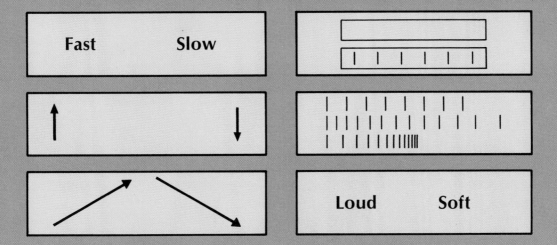

Follow the notes in the color blocks.

One shows the melody moving upward.

One shows the melody moving downward.

Where else does the melody move upward and downward?

RING GAME

FOLK TUNE FROM HAITI
COLLECTED AND ADAPTED BY CHARITY BAILEY
WORDS BY CARMINO RAVOSA

© 1972 CARMINO RAVOSA AND CHARITY BAILEY

There's a ring that's on the string,

And it's go - ing round and round.

And the ring that's on the string

Go - ing round must be found.

Fi - lé fi - lé fi - lé ba - gui - ni,

Fi - lé fi - lé ba - gui - ni, Oh!

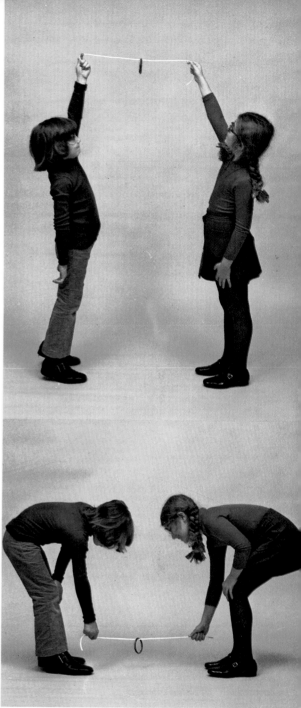

Now play a game that shows upward and downward.

These notes show downward direction in a melody.

Where do you hear them in the song?

THE DEATH OF MISTER FLY

FOLK SONG FROM POLAND   ENGLISH WORDS BY MARGARET MARKS

1.   Mister Fly climbed up a tree,

Cried, "I'm high as high can be!"

Lost his grip, came crashing down,

Smashed to pieces on the ground.

2.   When the insects heard the sound

Echoing for miles around,

They began to buzz and cry,

"Quick! First aid for Mister Fly!"

3.   "Where's a bandage?" "Where's a splint?"

"Get some liniment and lint!"

"Someone give him aspirin!"

"Should we call the doctor in?"

4.   Then a wise old flea spoke out,

"You don't know what you're about!

He's beyond the reach of aid,

Get a pick and get a spade!"

5.   Then at last those insects knew

What they really had to do!

Now his tombstone bears the scrawl:

"He who climbs too high must fall."

Play in an upward direction for the first two lines.

D F G A Repeat

Play in a downward direction for the last two lines.

G F E D Repeat

THE LITTLE TREE
FOLK SONG FROM SPAIN   ENGLISH WORDS BY ROSEMARY JACQUES

1. In a Span-ish gar-den stands a lit - tle tree;

In the spring-time it's a love - ly thing to see,

For it wears a coat of ___ bright - est green,

A brand new ___ coat of ___ bright - est green.

2. In a Spanish garden stands a little tree;
In the autumn it's a lovely thing to see,
For it wears a coat of shiny gold,
A brand new coat of shiny gold.

3. In a Spanish garden stands a little tree;
In the winter it's a lovely thing to see,
For it wears a coat of glist'ning white,
A winter coat of glist'ning white.

Follow the words in the color blocks.

Which arrow shows the direction you hear?

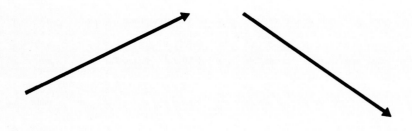

LITTLE BY LITTLE

WORDS BY CARMINO RAVOSA

© 1970 CARMINO RAVOSA

Little by, little by, little by, little by,
big things get done;
Little by, little by, little by, little by,
battles are won.

Little by, little by, little by, little by,
you'll reach the skies;
Little by, little by, little by, little by
you'll take the prize.

Little by, little by, smile by smile,
Inch by inch and mile by mile,
Little by, little by, little by, little by, lot.

Follow the words in the color blocks.

Which arrow shows the direction you hear?

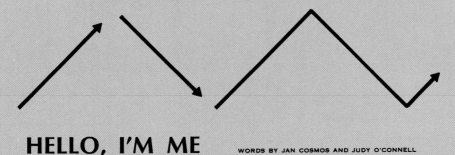

HELLO, I'M ME

WORDS BY JAN COSMOS AND JUDY O'CONNELL

Hello, I'm me, And lucky as can be,

For I can learn and play and grow, you see.

Growing strong and growing tall;

A little while, I won't be small;

Running, reaching for the sun,

just look at me because

I'm me, I'm me, And lucky as can be,

For I can learn and play and grow, you see.

Arms and legs and feet for running free.

Hands that make, Eyes that see.

A heart that loves. Wheeeeeeee! Lucky me.

Hello, I'm me, And lucky as can be,

For I can learn and play and grow, you see.

Growing strong and growing tall;

A little while, I won't be small;

Running, reaching for the sun,

just look at me because I'm me.

TONE COLOR

SOUND PIECE 3: A Little Farm Talk ELIZABETH CROOK

Make up some music of animal sounds.

Will you use high or low sounds?

long or short sounds?

loud or soft sounds?

What tempo will you use?

THE BARNYARD

WORDS BY CARMINO RAVOSA

1. Barnyard, barnyard, all around the barnyard,

    Hear the cow go, "Moo, moo."

    Barnyard, barnyard, all around the barnyard,

    Hear the duck go, "Quack, quack."

    All around the barnyard,

    Animals are talking;

    Though it sounds to you like

    Just a lot of squawking.

    Barnyard, barnyard, all around the barnyard,

    Hear the goose go, "Honk, honk."

    Barnyard, barnyard, all around the barnyard,

    Hear the chicken, "Cluck, cluck, Cluck, cluck."

2. Barnyard, barnyard, all around the barnyard,

    Hear the pig go, "Oink, oink."

    Barnyard, barnyard, all around the barnyard,

    Hear the sheep go, "Baa, baa."

    All around the barnyard,

    Animals are talking;

    Though it sounds to you like

    Just a lot of squawking.

    Barnyard, barnyard, all around the barnyard,

    Hear the horse go, "Neigh, neigh."

    Barnyard, barnyard, all around the barnyard,

    Hear the donkey, "Hee-haw, Hee-haw."

Play on all animal sounds:

F♯   G

79

Say this poem.

Use the tone color of your voice.

THE HOUSE CAT

The house cat sits
And smiles and sings.
He knows a lot
Of secret things.

Annette Wynne

Now use your voice in a different way.

How will you say the poem now?

SOUND PIECE 4: The House Cat   DAVID S. WALKER

THE HOUSE CAT SITS
AND SMILES AND SINGS.
HE KNOWS A LOT OF
SECRET THINGS

Each musical instrument has its own *tone color*.

Can you tell each instrument by its sound?

Listen to the recording.

Which sound goes with which picture?

piano

trumpet

clarinet

string bass

temple blocks

83

In which sections do you see pictures of instruments, A or B?

Listen for the instruments in the A sections.

Listen for the silence in the B section.

Can you think of a way to fill in the silence in section B?

Which tone colors will you choose?

Will you use your voice?

Will you use an instrument?

Will you use a sound in the room?

Will you use a sound like clapping or snapping?

THE ARTS: SEEING AND HEARING

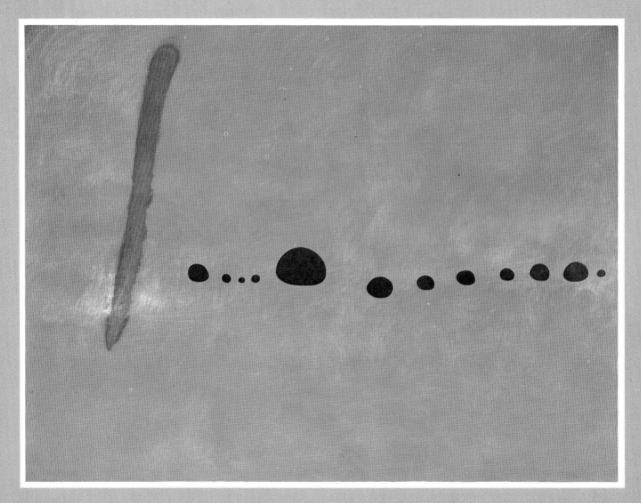

Miró. BLUE II.

What part of you lets you enjoy a painting?

Ears? Nose? Eyes? Fingers? Tongue?

What part of you lets you enjoy music?

Ears? Nose? Eyes? Fingers? Tongue?

METER IN TWO AND THREE

Sing, play, or move to something in *twos*.

Old Mother Witch

(page 44)

Tue, Tue

The Critter Got Away

The Band in the Square

Shoo, Fly

The Frog Song

Sing, play, or move to something in *threes*.

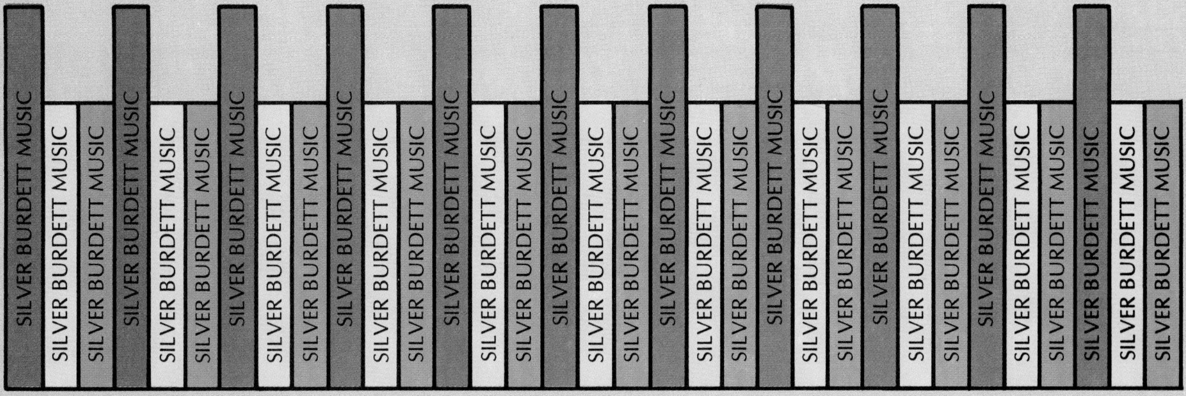

Old Mother Witch

(page 45)

Sommer, Ade

Sheep Shearing

The Village Dance

Pockets

Show beats grouped in sets of three.

Will you sing, play, or move?

ALPHABET SONG FOLK SONG FROM NEWFOUNDLAND

From Songs of the Newfoundland Outports, Vol. 1, by Kenneth Peacock. Queen's Printer 1965.

The National Museum of Man of The National Museums of Canada. Reproduced by permission of the Minister of Supply and Services Canada.

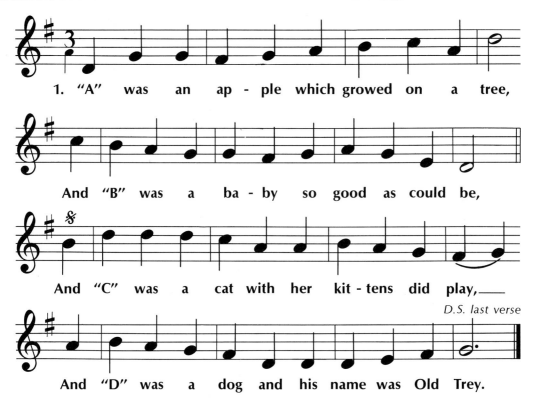

1. "A" was an ap - ple which growed on a tree,

And "B" was a ba - by so good as could be,

And "C" was a cat with her kit - tens did play,——

D.S. last verse

And "D" was a dog and his name was Old Trey.

2. "E" was an eagle so fierce and so free,

   And "F" was a fish deep down in the sea,

   And "G" was a goat with her gamboling tricks,

   And "H" was a hen with her dear little chicks.

3. "I" was an isle where no prayer could I hear,

    And "J" was a jug full of water so clear,

    And "K" was a kite flew high in the air,

    And "L" was a lion just come out from the lair.

4. "M" was a moth through the flame it did fly,

    And "N" was a nest where six pretty eggs lie,

    And "O" was an ox who loved grass and fresh hay,

    And "P" was a pig fond of eating all day.

5. "Q" is our Queen and long may she live,

    And "R" was a robin some crumbs may she give,

    And "S" was a swan with her white downy wing,

    And "T" was a tulip first out in the spring.

6. "U" was umbrella to shelter from rain,

    And "V" was a vase sweet flowers to contain,

    And "W" was a watch ladies wear by their side,

    And "X" was the Cross on which a good man had died,

    And "Y" was the yoke on the neck for to place,

    And "Z" was a zebra just come from the race.

Play the bells high or low.

Play when the first letter of your name is sung.

Add finger cymbals to this carol.

Play long sounds.

3 𝅗𝅥. | 𝅗𝅥. | 𝅗𝅥. ' | 𝅗𝅥. :‖ Repeat through the song.

LULLABY POLISH CAROL   ENGLISH WORDS BY TULLA STATLER

1. What shall__ I bring to the Babe in the__ man-ger,

So He'll__ not cry when He wakes from His sleep?__

I'll bring Him__ ap - ples__ as__ gold - en as sun-light,

Lul - la - by, Je - sus, oh, please do not weep.__

2. What shall I bring to the Mother who rocks Him,
   Holding Him close in Her arms as He sleeps?
   I'll bring Her pears fresh and bright as the morning,
   Lullaby, Jesus, oh, please do not weep.

Which section has beats grouped in twos?

Which section has beats grouped in threes?

The notation will tell you.

DIPIDU
FOLK SONG FROM UGANDA   ENGLISH WORDS BY JOAN GILBERT VAN POZNAK

FROM UNICEF BOOK OF CHILDREN'S SONGS. COMPILED AND WITH PHOTOGRAPHS BY WILLIAM I. KAUFMAN. COPYRIGHT 1970 BY WILLIAM I. KAUFMAN. PUBLISHED BY STACKPOLE BOOKS.

Good-day, good-day to you, Good-day, O dip-i-du,

Good-day, good-day to you, Good-day, O dip-i-du.

Dip, dip, dip-i-du, Dip-i-du, O dip-i-du.

Dip, dip, dip dip, dip-i-du, Dip-i-du, O dip-i-du.

RHYTHM PATTERN

Words have patterns.

Do the words in this poem have long sounds, short sounds,

or both?

LAZY JANE

Shel Silverstein

Lazy __ __
lazy __ __
lazy __ __
lazy __ __
lazy __ __
lazy __ __
Jane, ____
she
wants
a
drink
of
water
so
she
waits ____
and __
waits ____
and __
waits ____
and __
waits ____
and __
waits ____
for
it
to
rain.

Find a word with a long sound.

Find a word with short sounds.

Find the word with the longest sounds.

Find the word with the shortest sounds.

Choose Group 1 or Group 2.

Use the tone color of your voice to perform "Bellabong."

SOUND PIECE 5: Bellabong DORIS HAYS

© 1979 QUINSKA/HAYS USED BY PERMISSION OF DORIS HAYS

	SLOW Like big bells Repeat many times		FAST Like small bells Repeat many times		FASTER Like small bells Repeat many times	
Group 1	BING BONG		Ping Ping Pong Pong		Sing Sing Song Song	⌢ LONG
Group 2		⌢ BONG		⌢ BONG		⌢ BONG

	Hold as long as you can		Hold as long as you can		Hold as long as you can

95

There is pattern in MOVEMENT.

Find the lines that show

the pattern of hop, run, and skip.

Hop ──── ──── ──── ────

Run ─ ─ ─ ─ ─ ─ ─ ─

Skip ── · ── · ── · ── ·

Notes can show the rhythm pattern
of each movement.

Hop

Run

Skip

Play one of the patterns on an instrument.

Ask a friend to move to the pattern you play.

Listen for a rhythm pattern in this music.

It is played on a tambourine.

Find the notes that show the pattern you heard.

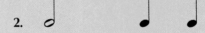

4.

Here are other rhythm patterns.

Can you play them on a tambourine?

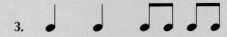

Music has rhythm pattern.

How many times can you find ♩ ♩ ♩?

Sing the pattern each time you see it.

HOP, OLD SQUIRREL BLACK-AMERICAN SINGING GAME

FROM ON THE TRAIL OF NEGRO FOLK-SONGS BY DOROTHY SCARBOROUGH. COPYRIGHT, 1925, BY HARVARD UNIVERSITY PRESS; 1953 BY MARY McDANIEL PARKER. REPRINTED BY PERMISSION.

1. Hop, old squirrel, ei - dle - dum, ei - dle - dum,

Hop, old squirrel, ei - dle - dum dum,

Hop, old squirrel, ei - dle - dum, ei - dle - dum,

Hop, old squirrel, ei - dle - dum dee.

2. Jump, old squirrel, eidledum, eidledum,
   Jump, old squirrel, eidledum dum,
   Jump, old squirrel, eidledum, eidledum,
   Jump, old squirrel, eidledum dee.

3. Run, old squirrel,

4. Hide, old squirrel,

Play the pattern on an A bell.

Look at the rhythm pattern in the color blocks.

♩ ♫ ♩ ♩

How do you think it will sound?

Sing it each time you see it.

FISHPOLE SONG

SOUTHERN SINGING GAME

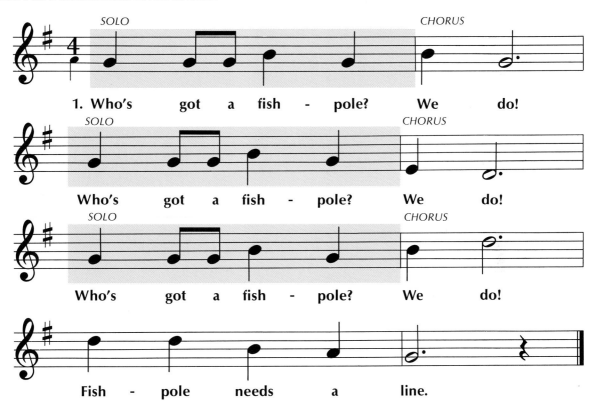

1. Who's got a fish - pole? We do!

Who's got a fish - pole? We do!

Who's got a fish - pole? We do!

Fish - pole needs a line.

2. Who's got a fishline? } *3 times*
   We do!

   Fishline needs a hook.

3. Who's got a fishhook? } *3 times*
   We do!

   Fishhook needs some bait.

4. Who's got a cricket? } *3 times*
   We do!

   Cricket catch a fish!

Each line of this song has the same rhythm pattern.

Clap the pattern as you listen.

AY-LYE, LYU-LYE   YIDDISH FOLK SONG   ENGLISH WORDS BY RICHARD MORRIS

REPRINTED BY PERMISSION OF SCHOCKEN BOOKS INC. FROM A TREASURY OF JEWISH FOLKSONG EDITED BY RUTH RUBIN. COPYRIGHT © 1950 BY SCHOCKEN BOOKS INC. COPYRIGHT RENEWED © 1978 BY RUTH RUBIN.

1. Ay - lye, lyu - lye, lyu - lye,

Go   to sleep now, don't   cry;

Close your eyes   in slum - ber,

Oh,   my   dar - ling kind' - lach.

2. Very soon I'll wake you,
   To the fair I'll take you;
   There'll be joy and laughter,
   Oh, my darling kind'lach.

3. You will find such treats there,
   Such good things to eat there;
   Rolls with apple butter,
   Oh, my darling kind'lach.

4. There will be a contest,
   Prizes for the finest
   Cows and horses entered,
   Oh, my darling kind'lach.

5. Papa's hoping we can
   Win a bright blue ribbon
   For our brand new heifer,
   Oh, my darling kind'lach.

6. Ay-lye, lyu-lye, lyu-lye,
   Go to sleep now, don't cry;
   Close your eyes in slumber,
   Oh, my darling kind'lach.

DREYDL SONG

FOLK SONG FROM ISRAEL   ENGLISH WORDS BY ROSEMARY JACQUES

A rhythm pattern is used many times in this song.
Listen for the rhythm pattern.

Chanukah, days of joy,

Happy time for girls and boys;

Glowing lights, joyous sounds,

Dreydl spinning round and round.

It reminds us of the glory

Of the days of Judah Maccabee;

Spin the dreydl, tell the story,

Oh, what fun for you and me.

Listen for the rhythm pattern of "Yum-pa-pa."
You will hear it in the B section of the song.

Clap "Yum-pa-pa" every time it comes in the song.
Can you make the "Yum-pa-pa" sound by stamping your feet?
Stamp one foot after the other.
Find the notes in the song that show this rhythm pattern.

A HAPPY SONG

FOLK SONG FROM ISRAEL   ENGLISH VERSION BY ROSEMARY JACQUES

FROM HI, NEIGHBOR (BOOK 2) BY UNITED STATES COMMITTEE FOR UNICEF, UNITED NATIONS, N.Y. USED BY PERMISSION.

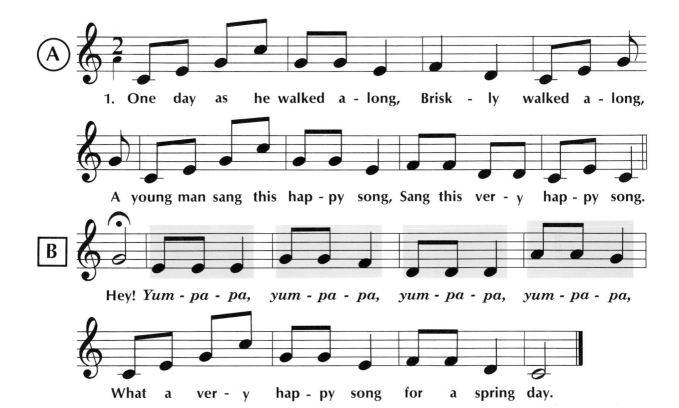

1. One day as he walked a-long, Brisk-ly walked a-long,

A young man sang this hap-py song, Sang this ver-y hap-py song.

Hey! *Yum-pa-pa, yum-pa-pa, yum-pa-pa, yum-pa-pa,*

What a ver-y hap-py song for a spring day.

2. Soon he met a maiden fair,

    Met a maiden fair;

    The young man tipped his hat to her,

    Shyly tipped his hat to her.

    Hey! *Yum-pa-pa, yum-pa-pa, yum-pa-pa, yum-pa-pa,*

    Young man tipped his hat to her on a spring day.

3. "Pretty maiden, let us dance,

    Round and round we'll whirl;

    Pretty maiden, let us dance,"

    Said the young man to the girl.

    Hey! *Yum-pa-pa, yum-pa-pa, yum-pa-pa, yum-pa-pa,*

    Round and round the town they whirled on a spring day.

THE ARTS: REPETITION

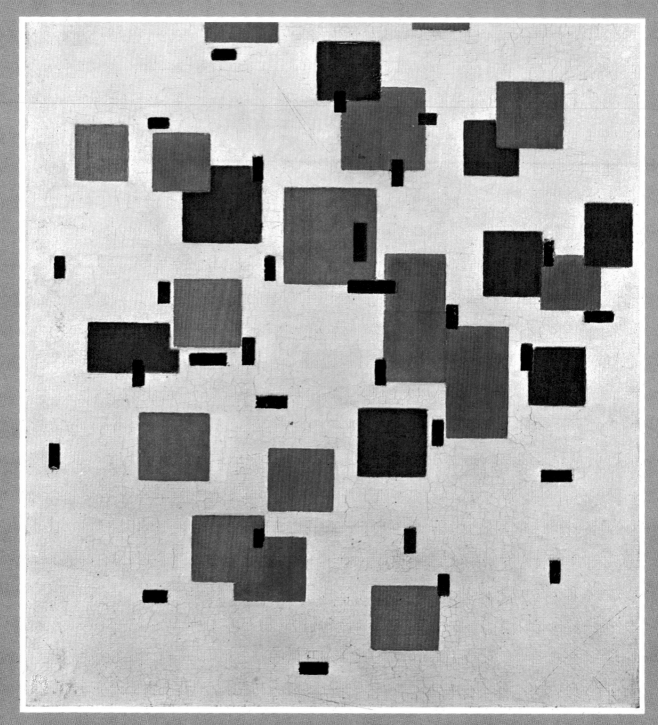

MONDRIAN: COMPOSITION IN BLUE B.

What repeats in this painting?

What repeats in the mask?

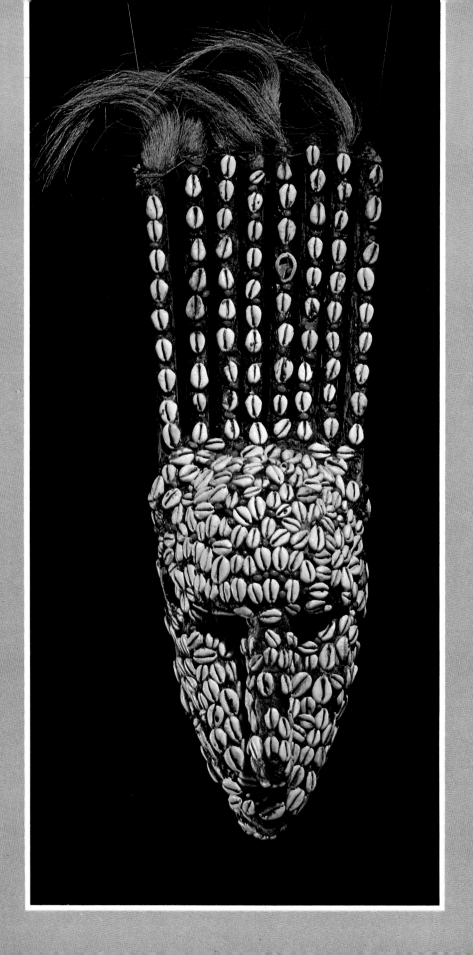

PHRASES

The pictures will help you do the motions for the singing game from Africa.

CHE CHE KOOLAY

As you sing the song, follow the *phrase lines.*

Are the phrases long, or short?

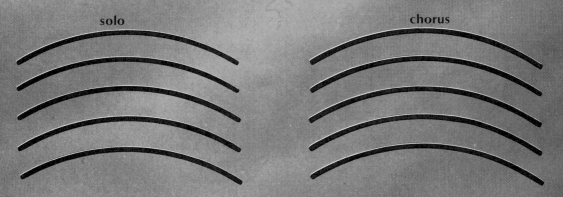

solo   chorus

Take turns singing the solo phrases and the chorus phrases.

CAN YOU DO THIS?

Follow the phrase lines as you sing the song.

Are the phrases the same length, or different?

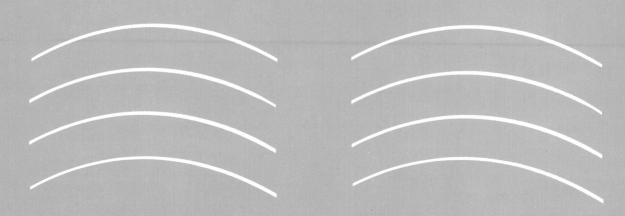

Choose a leader to move on the solo phrases.

All follow on the chorus phrases.

Make your motion last all through each phrase.

solo   chorus

Leader make up a motion.   All follow.

Leader make up a motion.   All follow.

Leader make up a motion.   All follow.

Leader make up a motion.   All follow.

Sing this song with the recording.

Follow the phrase lines as you sing.

Are there short phrases, long phrases, or both?

MARY HAD A BABY BLACK SPIRITUAL

1. Mar - y had a ba - by, Yes, Lord!

Mar - y had a ba - by, Yes, my Lord!

Mar - y had a ba - by, Yes, Lord!

The peo - ple keep a - com - in' an' the train done gone.

2. What did She name Him?
   Yes, Lord!
   What did She name Him?
   Yes, my Lord!
   What did She name Him?
   Yes, Lord!
   The people keep a-comin' an' the train done gone.

3. Named Him King Jesus,

4. Where was He born?

5. Born in a stable,

109

Sometimes poems use short phrases and long phrases.

Look at this poem.

Can you find short phrases?

Can you find long phrases?

SUMMER SONG

By the sand between my toes,

By the waves behind my ears,

By the sunburn on my nose,

By the little salty tears

That make rainbows in the sun

When I squeeze my eyes and run,

By the way the seagulls screech,

Guess where I am? *At the* . . . . . !

By the way the children shout,

Guess what happened? *School is* . . . . . !

By the way I sing this song

Guess if summer lasts too long:

You must answer Right or . . . . . !

John Ciardi

There are short and long phrases in "Bye'm Bye."

Feel the many short phrases and the one long one.

BYE'M BYE   FOLK SONG FROM TEXAS

Bye'm bye, Bye'm bye, Stars shin-ing,

Num-ber, num-ber one, num-ber two,

num-ber three, num-ber four, num-ber five,

Oh, my! Bye'm bye, bye'm bye, Oh, my! Bye'm bye.

USING WHAT YOU KNOW ABOUT MUSIC

Look at the rhythm pattern in the color blocks.

Can you find the same pattern in other places?

Follow the notes as you sing "Nu Ja Ja."

NU JA JA   SILESIAN FOLK SONG   ENGLISH WORDS BY TRUDI EICHENLAUB

1. Rös - el, when you mar - ry me, *Nu ja ja, nu ja ja!*

I'll be hap - py as can be, *Nu ja ja, ja!*

2. Josef, when you marry me,
   Nu ja ja, nu ja ja!
   Oh, how very proud I'll be,
   Nu ja ja, ja!

3. Rösel, dear, when you are mine,
   You'll do my bidding all the time.

4. If your bidding I must do,
   Then I will not marry you.

5. Rösel, dear, that's fine with me,
   Other fish are in the sea.

IN THE WINDOW

JEWISH FOLK MELODY   ENGLISH WORDS BY JUDITH K. EISENSTEIN

"MY CANDLES," FROM THE GATEWAY TO JEWISH SONG. COPYRIGHT 1939 BY BEHRMAN'S JEWISH BOOK HOUSE, NEW YORK. USED BY PERMISSION

1. In the win - dow, where you can send your glow
From my Me - no - rah on new - ly fall - en snow,
I will set you one lit - tle can - dle
On this the first night of Cha - nu - kah.

2. In the window, where you can send your glow

From my Menorah on newly fallen snow,

I will set you two little candles

On this the second night of Chanukah.

3. . . . three . . . third . . .

4. . . . four . . . fourth . . .

5. . . . five . . . fifth . . .

6. . . . six . . . sixth . . .

7. . . . seven . . . seventh . . .

8. . . . eight . . .eighth . . .

113

OLD JOE CLARK

AMERICAN FOLK SONG

Play Section A.

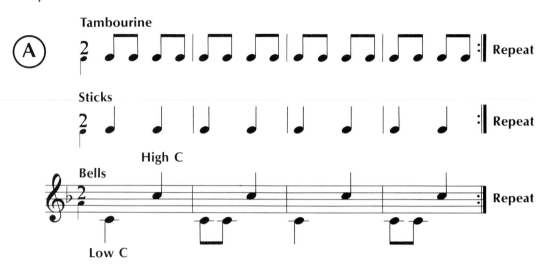

Tambourine

(A)

Repeat

Sticks

Repeat

Bells

High C

Low C

Repeat

Sing as you move in Section B.

B

Rock-a-rock, Old Joe Clark,

Rock-a-rock, I'm gone;

Rock-a-rock, Old Joe Clark,

Good-by, Lucy Long.

Follow the phrase lines as you listen to "Hato Popo."

Are the phrases the same length, or different?

HATO POPO

FOLK SONG FROM JAPAN

Po - po - po! Ha - to po - po!

Ma - me ga ho - shi - i - ka? So - ra ya - ru zo!

Min - na - de na - ka - yo - ku, Ta - be - ni ko - i.

As you listen, follow the notes to discover the rhythm pattern.

GREAT BIG STARS BLACK SPIRITUAL

1. Great big stars 'way up___ yon - der,

Great big stars 'way up___ yon - der,

Great big stars 'way up___ yon - der,

Oh, my lit - tle soul's gon - na shine, shine!

Oh, my lit - tle soul's gon - na shine, shine!

2. Great big stars 'way up yonder, (*3 times*)

   All around the world gonna shine, shine! (*2 times*)

Listen to the recording.

You will hear a rhythm pattern. ♩♫♫

It is played on a tambourine.

When you sing, feel the short phrases and the long phrases.

Add a cymbal at the end of each phrase.

Play the cymbal when you see .

BATTLE HYMN OF THE REPUBLIC

MUSIC BY WILLIAM STEFFE
WORDS BY JULIA WARD HOWE

Glo - ry, glo - ry, hal - le - lu - jah!

Glo - ry, glo - ry, hal - le - lu - jah!

Glo - ry, glo - ry, hal - le - lu - jah! His truth is march-ing on.

MY NIPA HUT

Which section has beats grouped in twos?

Which section has beats grouped in threes?

The notation will tell you.

A   Which parts will match Section A?

LITTLE BULL

FOLK SONG FROM LATIN AMERICA   ENGLISH WORDS BY A. H. GREEN

1. Hey,__ lit-tle bull be-hind the gate, What are you do-ing up so late?

And,__ lit-tle bull, what have you seen   On this__ star-ry__ Christ-mas E'en?

If   you raise your eyes to heav-en, you will see the Vir-gin's Son.

He   is clothed in white ap-par-el   and   is bless-ing ev-'ry-one.

La la la la la   la   la   la   la,   La   la   la   la la la la la la la;

La la la la la   la   la la   la,   La   la la la   la la la   la la.

2.   Hey, little bull behind the gate,

What are you doing up so late?

And, little bull, what have you seen

On this starry Christmas E'en?

Forward, forward, little shepherd, march on bravely, ev'ryone,

Thanking God with hearts o'erflowing for the gift of His blessed Son.

La la la la la . . .

119

The record players look different.
They are in different *styles*.

The cars look different.
They are in different *styles*.

The hats look different.
They are in different *styles*.

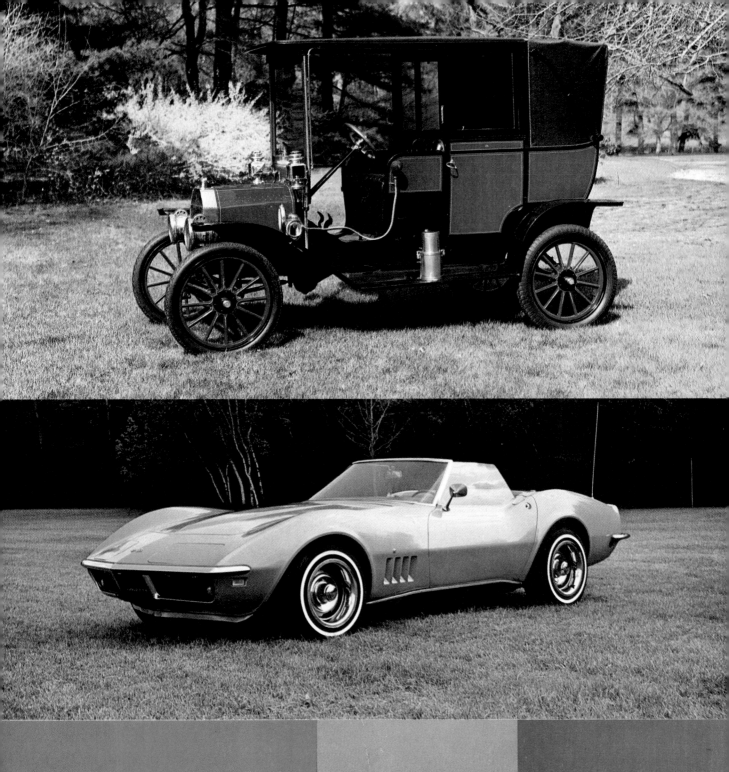

Can you think of other
things that are in
different styles?

INTERVALS

Find things that show leaps, steps, and repeats.

Find some of the parts you have played.

Which ones use repeated tones?

Which ones use steps?

Which ones use leaps?

Which ones use repeats and leaps?

D E F# E D
Hal - le - lu - jah.

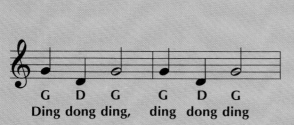

G D G   G D G
Ding dong ding,   ding dong ding

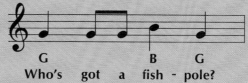

G   B   G
Who's got a fish - pole?

B A G
sum-mer day

B A G F   E D C
smashed to pie - ces   on the ground

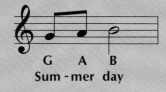

G A B
Sum - mer day

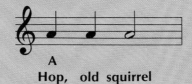

A
Hop, old squirrel

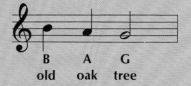

G A B   B A G
La - dy, come   old oak tree

Look at the notes in the color blocks.

Do the notes step, leap, or repeat?

JOHN THE RABBIT
AMERICAN FOLK GAME SONG • COLLECTED BY JOHN W. WORK

Old John the rab-bit, Oh, yes! Old John the rab-bit, Oh, yes!

Got a might-y bad hab-it, Oh, yes! Of go-ing to my gar-den, Oh, yes!

And eat-ing up my peas, Oh, yes! And cut-ting down my cab-bage, Oh, yes!

He ate to-ma-toes, Oh, yes! And sweet po-ta-toes, Oh, yes!

And if I live, Oh, yes! To see next fall, Oh, yes!

I won't plant, Oh, yes! A gar-den at all!

Find the notes that repeat in the blue color blocks.

Find the notes that leap.

ONE COLD AND FROSTY MORNING
BLACK-AMERICAN FOLK SONG

"OLD JESSE" FROM ON THE TRAIL OF NEGRO FOLK-SONGS BY DOROTHY SCARBOROUGH.
COPYRIGHT, 1925, BY HARVARD UNIVERSITY PRESS; 1953 BY MARY McDANIEL PARKER. REPRINTED BY PERMISSION.

One cold and frost-y morn-ing just as the sun did rise,

The pos-sum roared, the rac-coon howled, 'cause he be-gan to freeze,

He drew him-self up in a knot, with his knees up to his chin,

And ev-'ry-thing had to clear the track when he stretched out a-gain.

Old Jes-se was a good man a-mong the old-en times.

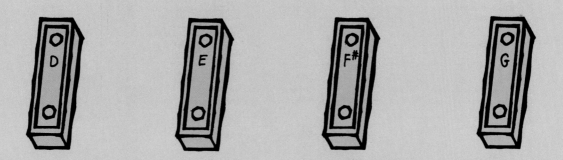

Find the notes that move by step.

Look in the color blocks.

WHOA, MULE! BLACK-AMERICAN FOLK SONG

FROM ON THE TRAIL OF NEGRO FOLK-SONGS BY DOROTHY SCARBOROUGH.
COPYRIGHT, 1925, BY HARVARD UNIVERSITY PRESS; 1953 BY MARY MCDANIEL PARKER. REPRINTED BY PERMISSION.

Whoa, mule, whoa, mule, whoa, mule, I tell you, Whoa, mule, I say!

Tied a slip-knot in his tail And his head slipped through the col-lar.

Hur-ry, hur-ry, save us, Hee-haw, hee-haw, hee-haw!

Hur-ry, hur-ry, save us! Whoa, mule, I say!

REFRAIN
Whoa, mule, I tell you, Whoa, mule, I say!

Ain't got time to kiss you now,

But don't you run a-way.

Which color block shows notes that REPEAT?

Which color block shows notes that LEAP?

Which color block shows notes that STEP and REPEAT?

THE ALLEE ALLEE O! GAME SONG FROM MASSACHUSETTS

FROM SINGING GAMES AND PLAYPARTY GAMES BY RICHARD CHASE. DOVER PUBLICATIONS, INC. NEW YORK. 1967. REPRINTED THROUGH PERMISSION OF THE PUBLISHER.

Find the notes that show REPEATS and STEPS.

Look in the blue color blocks.

ROCKY MOUNTAIN

SOUTHERN FOLK SONG

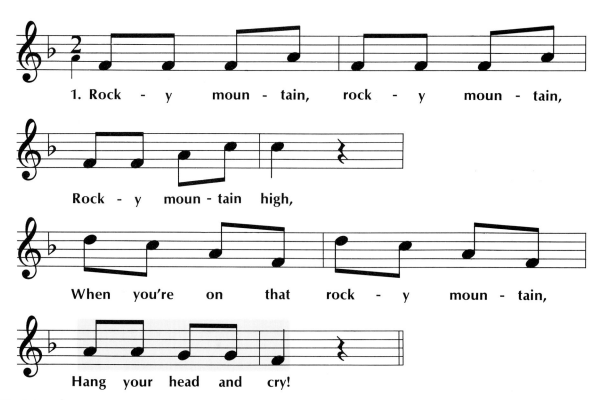

1. Rock - y   moun - tain,   rock - y   moun - tain,

Rock - y   moun - tain high,

When   you're   on   that   rock - y   moun - tain,

Hang   your   head   and   cry!

Find the notes that show LEAPS upward.

look in the red color blocks.

Find the one STEP upward in the red color blocks.

REFRAIN

Do, do, do, do,

Do re - mem - ber me;

Do, do, do, do,

Do re - mem - ber me.

2. Sunny valley, sunny valley,

   Sunny valley low,

   When you're in that

   Sunny valley,

   Sing it soft and slow. *Refrain*

3. Stormy ocean, stormy ocean,

   Stormy ocean wide;

   When you're on that

   Deep blue sea,

   There's no place you can hide. *Refrain*

Do the notes in this song mostly step, leap, or repeat?

CROOKED LITTLE MAN
WORDS AND MUSIC BY ERSEL HICKEY AND ED E. MILLER

There was a crook-ed man and he had a crook-ed smile;

Had a crook-ed six-pence and he walked a crook-ed mile.

Had a crook-ed cat and he had a crook-ed mouse;

They all lived to-geth-er in a crook-ed lit-tle house.

B Oh no, oh no, don't let the rain come down,

Oh no, don't let the rain come down,

Oh no, don't let the rain come down,

My roof's got a hole in it and I might drown,

Oh yes, my roof's got a hole in it and I might drown.

Sing the words *bobbidi boo*.

Do the notes move by step or by leap?

What do the arrows show?

Find the notes that match the arrows in section B.

BIBBIDI BOBBIDI BOO WORDS BY MACK DAVID, AL HOFFMAN, AND JERRY LIVINGSTON

A

If your mind is in a dither, and your heart is in a haze,

I'll haze your dither and dither your haze,

With a magic phrase.

If you're chased around by trouble, and you're followed by a jinx,

I'll jinx your trouble and trouble your jinx in less than forty winks.

B ‖: Salagadoola menchicka boola,

bib - bi - di bob - bi - di boo,

Put 'em to - geth - er and what have you got?   Bib - bi - di bob - bi - di boo.

Salagadoola means menchicka booleroo,

But the thing-a-ma-bob that does the job is bibbidi bobbidi boo.

Salagadoola menchicka boola,

bib - bi - di bob-bi - di boo,

Put 'em to - geth - er and what have you got?

Bibbidi bobbidi, bibbidi bobbidi,

bib - bi - di bob - bi - di boo.

131

THE ARTS: MATERIALS

THE WHITE WINDOW

The moon comes every night to peep

Through the window where I lie;

But I pretend to be asleep;

And watch the moon go slowly by.

    And she never makes a sound!

She stands and stares! And then she goes

To the house that's next to me,

Stealing by on tippy-toe;

To peep at folk asleep maybe.

    And she never makes a sound!

James Stephens

Each art has its special material.

What is the material of of painting?

          of dance?

          of poetry?

          of music?

CADENCE

Look at the end of section A.

The ending is called a *cadence*.

WILLOWBEE AMERICAN FOLK SONG

This way we wil-low-bee, oh, wil-low-bee, oh, wil-low-bee,

Oh, this way we wil-low-bee,___ All day___ long.

When you move, feel the strong cadence.

Find the cadence in section B.

Oh,___ Danc-ing down the al - ley, the al - ley, the al - ley,

Danc - ing down the al - ley, All day long. Oh,___

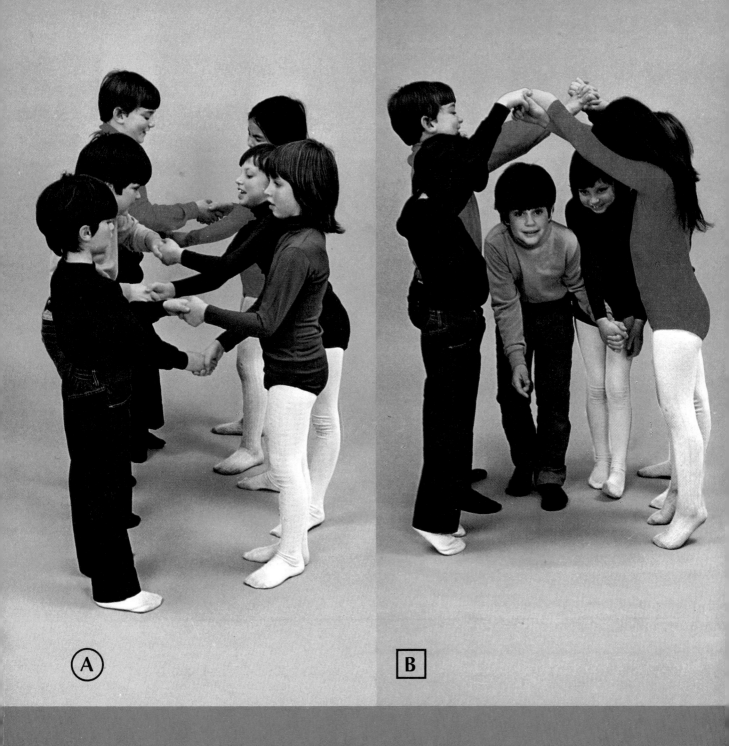

Feel the strong cadence when you "dance down the alley."

Which has a stronger cadence, the question part or the answer part?
Take turns singing the question and answer parts.

WHERE DO YOU GO?
FRENCH-CANADIAN FOLK SONG   ENGLISH WORDS BY ROSEMARY JACQUES

FROM JONGLEUR SONGS OF OLD QUEBEC, BY MARIUS BARBEAU. COPYRIGHT © 1962 BY RUTGERS, THE STATE UNIVERSITY. REPRINTED BY PERMISSION OF RUTGERS UNIVERSITY PRESS.

1. "Lit - tle boy, where do you go?

Lit - tle boy, where do you go?

Will you tell me as you pass____ by?"____

"Why, I'm off to school, of course,

Though I'd rath - er ride my horse,"

Was a young lad of sev - en's re - ply.

2. "What is higher than the trees? (*2 times*)

Will you tell me as you pass by?"

"Why, the sky that is so blue,

And the sun that shines there, too,"

Was a young lad of seven's reply.

3. "What things grow upon the earth? (*2 times*)

   Will you tell me as you pass by?"

   "Why, the oats and golden wheat

   That the cows and horses eat,"

   Was a young lad of seven's reply.

4. "When you're grown, what will you be? (*2 times*)

   Will you tell me as you pass by?"

   "Why, I'll be a farmer bold,

   It's a good life, I am told,"

   Was a young lad of seven's reply.

Which section in this song has a strong cadence? A or B?

ALL ME ROCK FOLK SONG FROM JAMAICA

WORDS AND MELODY FROM LULLABIES OF THE WORLD. ED. BY DOROTHY BERLINER COMMINS. COPYRIGHT © 1967 BY DOROTHY BERLINER COMMINS. REPRINTED BY PERMISSION OF RANDOM HOUSE, INC.

All me rock, me rock Boy - sie, Boy - sie would-n't sleep;

All me rock, me rock Boy - sie, Boy - sie would-n't sleep.

Go up town, go down town, See Boy - sie there.

Go up town, go down town, See Boy - sie there.

(A) Sing section A again.

The form is ABA.

Listen for the words that rhyme at the end of each phrase.

Which phrase has the strong cadence?

HUSH, LITTLE BABY   SOUTHERN FOLK SONG   COLLECTED BY JEAN RITCHIE

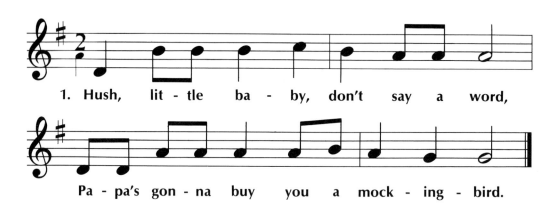

1. Hush, lit - tle ba - by, don't say a word,
Pa - pa's gon - na buy you a mock - ing - bird.

2. If that mockingbird won't sing,
   Papa's gonna buy you a di'mond ring.

3. If that di'mond ring turns to brass,
   Papa's gonna buy you a looking glass.

4. If that looking glass gets broke,
   Papa's gonna buy you a billy goat.

5. If that billy goat won't pull,
   Papa's gonna buy you a cart and bull.

6. If that cart and bull turn over,
   Papa's gonna buy you a dog named Rover.

7. If that dog named Rover won't bark,
   Papa's gonna buy you a horse and cart.

8. If that horse and cart fall down,
   You'll be the sweetest little one in town.

Add your own verse.

Think of words that sound alike.

Shake the tambourine after a strong cadence.

Strike the triangle after a weak cadence.

Listen before you choose which instrument to play.

WHO'LL BUY MY FRUIT? FOLK SONG FROM CZECHOSLOVAKIA   ENGLISH WORDS BY MARGARET MARKS

1., 2. Who'll come this way and buy?

Who'll buy my fruit piled high?
nuts

Peach - es, pears, and plums, and ap - ples,
Chest - nuts, wal - nuts, roast - ed al - monds,

Who'll come this way and buy?

If you try them, you will buy them.

Who'll come this way and buy?

The words in white show strong cadences.

Cadences in other phrases are weak.

NAUGHTY LITTLE FLEA

WORDS BY NORMAN THOMAS   TRANSCRIBED FROM THE RECORDING BY MIRIAM MAKEBA AND HARRY BELAFONTE

© 1957 PINEBROOK MUSIC CORP. C/O H/B WEBMAN & COMPANY USED BY PERMISSION

Refrain

Where did the naughty little flea go?

Won't somebody tell me?

Where did the naughty little flea go?

Won't somebody tell me?

1.   There was a naughty little flea;

He climbed upon the doggie's knee;

He climbed some here, he climbed some there;

He was climbing everywhere. Tell me,

Refrain

2.   He climbed some here, he climbed some there;

He was climbing everywhere.

And now at last he's found a nest

Where he can get some food and rest. Tell me,

Refrain

3.   He bit him here, he bit him there;

He bit him almost everywhere.

When he was done he wanted more;

He never tasted such a dog before. Tell me,

Refrain

RAID THE REFRIGERATOR

WORDS BY BOB SAKAYAMA

1. Mister Kangaroo was ridin' his bike,

    pumpin' on an uphill street;

    He said, "I know what I need now, I know what I'd like,

    I feel like havin' somethin' to eat.

    I've gotta go on home now and do it right away,

    You know I can't put it off till later;

    It just seems like the right thing to do today,

    I'm gonna raid that refrigerator;

    I'm gonna raid that refrigerator."

2. Mister Alligator was fishin' in the swamp,

    sittin', gettin' mud on his feet;

    He said, "I know what I need now, I know what I'd like,

    I feel like havin' somethin' to eat.

    I've gotta go on home now and do it right away,

    You know I can't put it off till later;

    It just seems like the right thing to do today,

    I'm gonna raid that refrigerator;

    I'm gonna raid that refrigerator."

3. Mister Hippopotamus was pullin' some weeds,

    pulled until his arms were beat;

    He said, 'I know what I need now, I know what I'd like,

    I feel like havin' somethin' to eat.

    I've gotta go on home now and do it right away,

    You know I can't put it off till later;

    It just seems like the right thing to do today,

    I'm gonna raid that refrigerator;

    I'm gonna raid that refrigerator."

RHYTHM PATTERN

Show rhythm pattern as you

MOVE PLAY SING

GOGO

SINGING GAME FROM KENYA   ENGLISH VERSION BY MARGARET MARKS   AS SUNG BY MARY OKARI

SOLO ... *CHORUS*

Turn out   your toe!   Cham - ni - a - mo   go - go.

SOLO ... *CHORUS*

And squat   down low!   Cham - ni - a - mo   go - go.

SOLO ... *CHORUS*

Now flap your arms and make a   face!   Cham - ni - a - mo   go - go.

SOLO ... *CHORUS*

And bump and clump a - bout the place!   Cham - ni - a - mo   go - go.

People in Africa play rhythm patterns in a special way.

Try one of the patterns.

Chant the numbers in each line.

Clap each time you say a large number.

Clap the second line as you listen to the recording.

1 2 **3** 4 **5** **6** 7 **8** 9 **10** 11 **12**

1 2 3 **4** 5 6 **7** 8 9 **10** 11 12

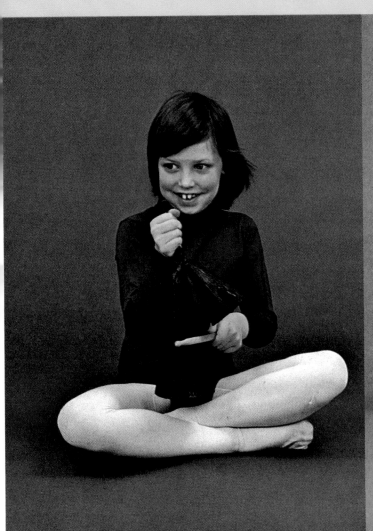

Look at the rhythm pattern in the color blocks.

Are they the same, or different?

CHRISTMAS BELLS

CHRISTMAS SONG FROM FRANCE   ENGLISH WORDS BY PAUL R. LADD

FROM CHRISTIAN LIFE IN SONG, COMPILED BY PAUL R. LADD, JR. REPRINTED BY PERMISSION OF SUMMY-BIRCHARD MUSIC.

Christ-mas bells are ring - ing; An - gels sing, "No - el!"

Praise and wel - come bring - ing To Em - man - u - el.

Christ-mas bells are ring - ing; An - gels sing, "No - el!"

Find a G bell.

Play the rhythm pattern as others sing.

Find a C bell.

Play the rhythm pattern as others sing.

Play both together with two mallets.

Play finger cymbals when you see ⨰ in the music.

SOUND PIECE 6: Rhythmpath   JOYCE BOGUSKY-REIMER

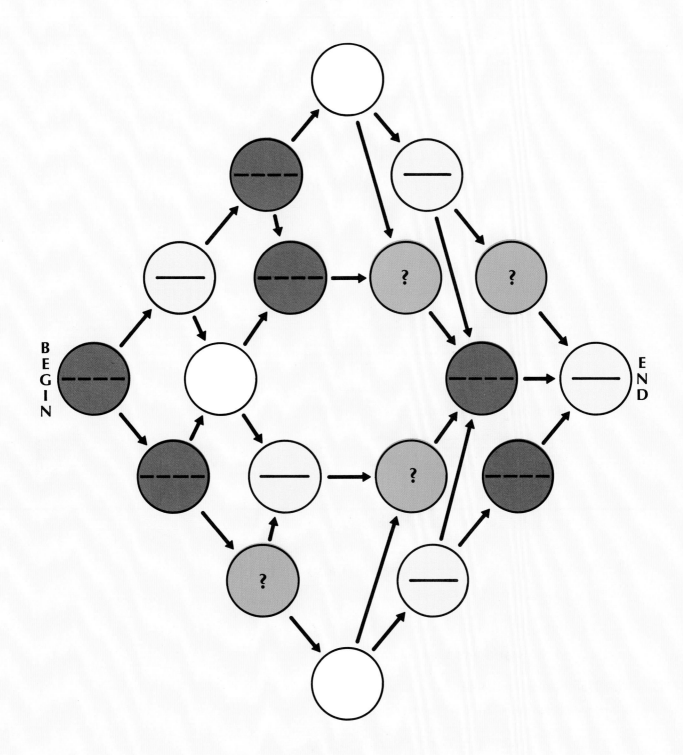

Many game songs use rhythm patterns.

Clap one of your own in "Hambone."

HAMBONE

AFRO-AMERICAN GAME SONG   WORDS BY CARMINO RAVOSA

USED BY PERMISSION.

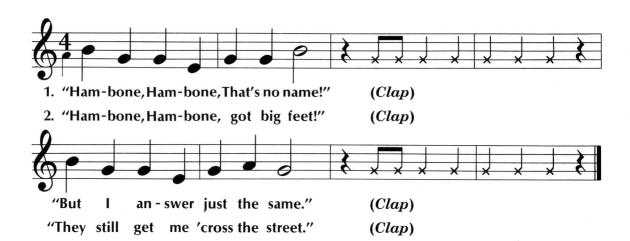

1. "Ham-bone, Ham-bone, That's no name!"   (*Clap*)

2. "Ham-bone, Ham-bone, got big feet!"   (*Clap*)

"But I an-swer just the same."   (*Clap*)

"They still get me 'cross the street."   (*Clap*)

3. "Hambone, Hambone, got no brain!" (*Clap*)

   "Still I keep out of the rain." (*Clap*)

4. "Hambone, Hambone, where you been?" (*Clap*)

   "Round the world and back again!" (*Clap*)

5. "Hambone, Hambone, don't cha smile?" (*Clap*)

   "Ev'ry little once in a while!" (*Clap*)

6. "Hambone, Hambone, don't cha cry?" (*Clap*)

   "When I get somethin' in my eye!" (*Clap*)

Ring, strike, or shake a rhythm pattern of your own.

WAKE, SNAKE   TRADITIONAL

Wake, snake, day is a - break - in',

Peas in the pot and the hoe cakes a - bak - in';

Green corn,

Use an instrument you ring.

Green corn,

Use an instrument you strike.

Green corn.

Use an instrument you shake.

Use what you know about
RHYTHM

Drum

Maracas

BE MY VALENTINE

FOLK SONG FROM PUERTO RICO   ENGLISH WORDS BY RUTH MARTIN

1. I was rid - ing through the mea - dows,

con el ¡ay! con el ¡ay, ay, ay!

On my bob - tail horse one day,

con el o - ri - qui - ti - tín, con el o - ri - qui - ti - tón.

2. When I met the Count's two daughters,
   con el ¡ay! con el ¡ay, ay, ay!
   As I went along the way,
   con el oriquititín, con el oriquititón.

3. Then I begged the youngest boldly,
   "Be my Valentine, I pray!"

4. And she said, "Yes, sir, I like you."
   "By your side I'll always stay."

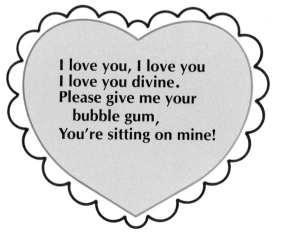

I love you, I love you
I love you divine.
Please give me your
   bubble gum,
You're sitting on mine!

148 Module 29: Review

Use what you know about

MELODY

THE UNBIRTHDAY SONG

WORDS AND MUSIC BY MACK DAVID, AL HOFFMAN, AND JERRY LIVINGSTON

Verse 1

A very merry unbirthday

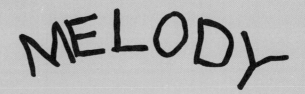

to you,   to you,

A very merry unbirthday

to you,   to you,

It's great to share with someone and

I guess that you will do.

A very merry unbirthday

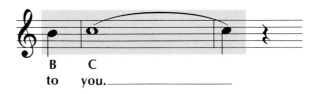

to you.

Verse 2

A very merry unbirthday

to us,   to us,

A very merry unbirthday

to us,   to us,

If there are no objections, let it be unanimous.

A very merry unbirthday

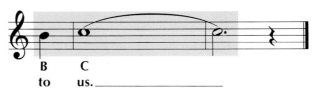

to us.

Look at the notes in the blue color blocks.

What do they tell you?

WINTER, ADE!   FOLK SONG FROM GERMANY   ENGLISH WORDS BY MARGARET MARKS

1. Win - ter, a - de!   Win - ter, a - de!

It may be sad to___ part, But laugh-ter fills my___ heart.

Win - ter, a - de!   Win - ter, a - de!

2. Winter, ade! Winter, ade!
   You can't stay round this place,
   Groundhog has shown his face.
   Winter, ade! Winter, ade!

3. Winter, ade! Winter, ade!
   To the North Pole with you!
   Stay there forever, do!
   Winter, ade! Winter, ade!

Now look at the notes in the red color block.

What do they tell you?

Sing "Garden Song."

Follow the phrases as you sing.

Some phrases are short. Some are long.

GARDEN SONG
WORDS BY DAVID MALLETT

Verse 1

Inch by inch, row by row,   gonna make this garden grow,

All it takes is a rake and a hoe and a piece of fertile ground.

Inch by inch, row by row,   someone bless the seeds I sow,

Someone warm them from below till the rain comes tumbling down.

Now listen for long and short phrases in other verses.

Verse 2

Pulling weeds and pickin' stones,   man is made of dreams and bones,

Feel the need to grow my own 'cause the time is close at hand.

Grain for grain, sun and rain,   find my way in nature's chain,

Tune my body and my brain to the music from the land.

Verse 3

Plant your rows straight and long,   temper them with prayer and song,

Mother Earth will make you strong if you give her love and care.

Old crow watching hungrily   from his perch in yonder tree,

In my garden I'm as free as that feathered thief up there.

(Repeat Verse 1)

Show tempo as you

ADIR HU   HEBREW SONG FROM YEMEN   ENGLISH VERSION BY DAVID BEN SHMUEL

God is great, God is Lord, Let us praise with one ac - cord.
A - dir hu, a - dir hu, yiv - ne vay - to b' - ka - rov.

He re - builds from the sand, Is - ra - el, our an - cient land.
Bim - heh - ra, bim - heh - ra, b' - ya - may - nu b' - ka - rov.

Then his chil - dren, then his chil - dren, then his chil - dren may re - turn.
Ayl b' - nay,___ ayl b' - nay, b' - nay vayt - cha ___ b' - ka - rov.

Then his chil - dren, then his chil - dren, then his chil - dren may re - turn.
Ayl b' - nay,___ ayl b' - nay, b' - nay vayt - cha ___ b' - ka - rov.

Listen to the recording of "Jesus Born in Bethlea."

Follow the phrase lines as you listen.

Are the phrases the same length, or different?

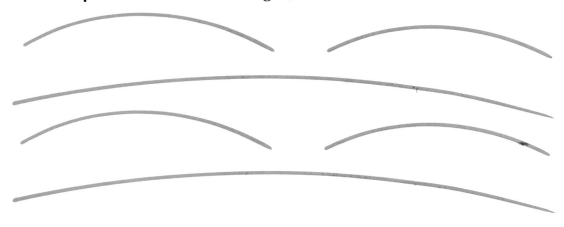

JESUS BORN IN BETHLEA

FOLK SONG FROM VIRGINIA

Transcribed and adapted from the Library of Congress field recording AFS 3160.

Je - sus born in Beth - lea, Je - sus born in Beth - lea,

Je - sus born in Beth - lea, and in the man - ger lay.

And in the man - ger lay, And in the man - ger lay,

Je - sus born in Beth - lea, and in the man - ger lay.

THE ARTS: VARYING AN IDEA

What is varied in these two paintings?

CHAGALL: THE VIOLINIST.
STEDELIJK MUSEUM, AMSTERDAM

HARMONY—NO HARMONY

Sometimes you hear melody alone.

1.

Sometimes you hear melody with *harmony*.

2.

Sing the melody alone, then add *harmony*.

COTTON-EYE JOE
FOLK SONG FROM TENNESSEE

TRANSCRIBED AND ADAPTED FROM THE LIBRARY OF CONGRESS FIELD RECORDING AFS 1619.

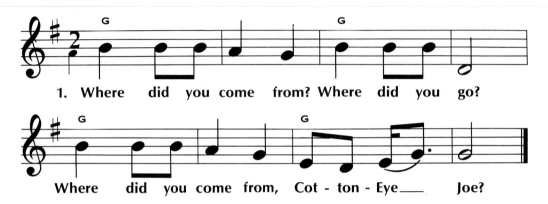

1. Where did you come from? Where did you go?

Where did you come from, Cot - ton - Eye___ Joe?

2. Come for to see you,

Come for to sing,

Come for to show you my diamond ring.

Play the bells or Autoharp as others sing.

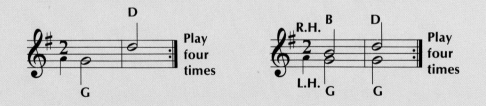

Which drawing shows what you hear?

1.

Melody alone

2.

Melody with harmony

Sing the melody alone, then add harmony.

HUSH-A-BA, BIRDIE FOLK SONG FROM SCOTLAND

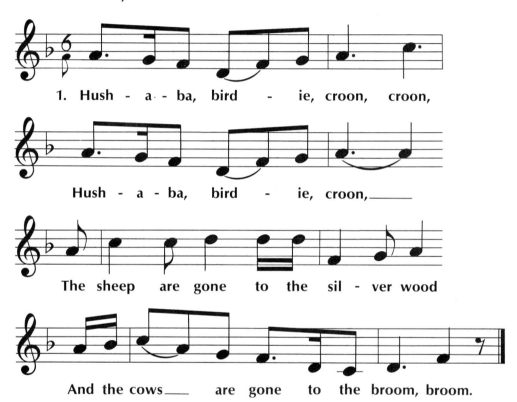

1. Hush - a - ba, bird - ie, croon, croon,

Hush - a - ba, bird - ie, croon,____

The sheep are gone to the sil - ver wood

And the cows____ are gone to the broom, broom.

2. Braw it is, milking the kye, kye,
   Braw it is, milking the kye,
   The birds are singing, the bells are ringing,
   And the wild deer come galloping by, by.

3. Hush-a-ba, birdie, croon, croon,
   Hush-a-ba, birdie, croon,
   The goats are gone to the mountains high
   And they'll not be home until noon, noon.

Play on bells.

1.

F D F

Play with two mallets together.

2.

R.H. C D C

L.H.

F

159

Sing this melody alone.

LADY, COME
FOLK SONG FROM ENGLAND

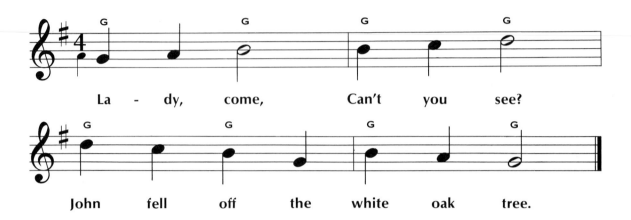

Lady, come, Can't you see?

John fell off the white oak tree.

Play a G chord on the Autoharp to add *harmony*.

Add another harmony part played on the bells.

Which one of these will you choose?

1. Low G A B

2. High D
Low D

3. High G

Which harmony part moves by step?

By leaps? By repeats?

Sing the melody alone.

BURNING LEAVES <small>"TAKIBI" ("BURNING LEAVES")</small>

All a - long the fence, the fence,

The cor - ner of the fence,

Burn - ing, burn - ing, burn - ing, burn - ing, see the burn - ing leaves.

Come and warm your hands, Hold them ver - y close.

Hear the North wind, oo,_____ blow - ing, blow - ing cold.

Add *harmony* by playing one of the bell parts.

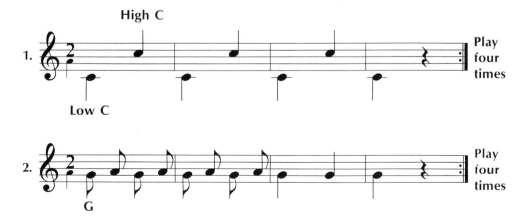

High C

1. Play four times

Low C

2. Play four times

G

Add harmony to melody by playing the bells.

Choose one of the color blocks.

Play it all the way through the song.

MORNING IS COME

TRADITIONAL   WORDS BY TRUDI EICHENLAUB

1. Come, sleep - y - heads,   O - pen   your   eyes;
2. Jump out   of   bed,   Do   not de - lay!

Bright sun   is shin - ing___ And___ blue are   the skies.
Don't want to   daw - dle___ On___ such   a   fine day.

Listen to *The Little Shepherd,* by Claude Debussy.

Instruments play a melody alone, then melody with harmony.

Play these parts on bells with "Hop Old Squirrel" (p. 98).

Play these parts on bells with "Fishpole Song" (p. 99).

What do the birds do all night long?

Sing the question as a melody alone.

ALL NIGHT LONG
MANX FOLK SONG   ENGLISH WORDS BY MARGARET MARKS

MELODY LINE FROM TWELVE MANX FOLK SONGS, BY MONA DOUGLAS AND ARNOLD FOSTER. PUBLISHED BY STAINER AND BELL, LONDON, 1926.

1. What do the birds do all night long, all night long,
all night long, What do the birds do all night long,
Af - ter I'm safe - ly tucked in? _____

2. What do the fish do all night long,
   all night long, all night long,
   What do the fish do all night long
   After I'm safely tucked in?

3. What do the cows do all night long,
   all night long, all night long,
   What do the cows do all night long
   After I'm safely tucked in?

4. What do the flow'rs do all night long,
   all night long, all night long,
   What do the flow'rs do all night long
   After I'm safely tucked in?

Add harmony for this section—the answer.

They sit on the branch-es the whole night through, whole night through,

whole night through, And ruf - fle their feath-ers a - gainst the dew

And wait for the day to be - gin._____

(2.) They swim to the depths of the silent lake,

silent lake, silent lake,

And under the cold rocks lie awake

And wait for the day to begin.

(3.) They huddle together beneath the trees,

'neath the trees, 'neath the trees,

And moo to the moon in the chill night breeze

And wait for the day to begin.

(4.) They fold up their petals and droop their heads,

droop their heads, droop their heads,

And patiently stand in their flower beds

And wait for the day to begin.

Play bells in this section.

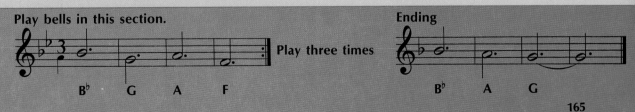

Play three times

Ending

B♭ G A F

B♭ A G

TONAL—ATONAL

Which drawing shows the arrows pointing to one place?

What does the other drawing show?

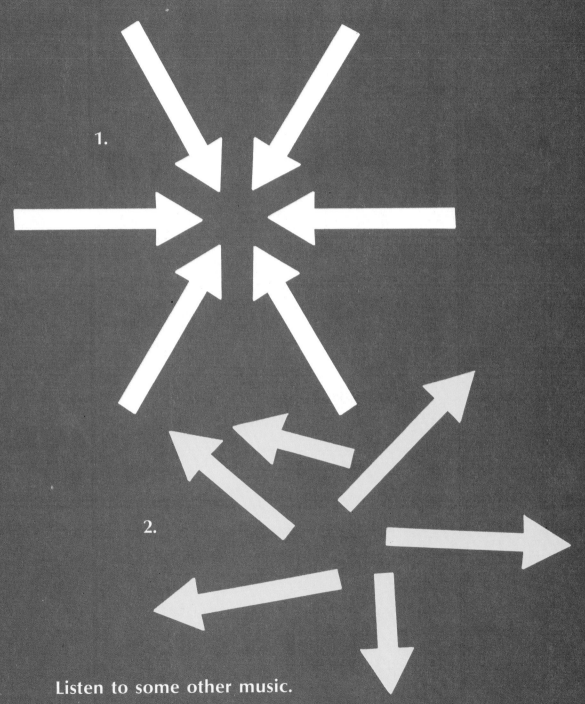

Listen to some other music.

Does it focus on one important tone, or not?

Which drawing seems to go with the music?

Does this song have an important ending tone?

THREE CRAW
FOLK SONG FROM SCOTLAND

1. Three craw sat up - on a wa',
Sat up-on a wa', Sat up-on a wa';_____
A B C#
Three craw sat up - on a wa',
On a cold and frost - y morn - ing.

2. The first craw couldna find his maw,

Couldna find his maw,

Couldna find his maw;

The first craw couldna find his maw,

On a cold and frosty morning.

3. The second craw couldna find his paw, . . .

4. The third craw ate the other twa, . . .

5. The fourth craw warna there at aw, . . .

6. And that's aw I hear about the craw, . . .

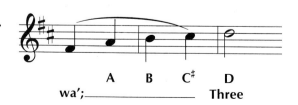

A B C# D

wa';_____ Three

Clap the rhythm of these words.

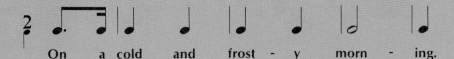

On   a cold   and   frost - y   morn - ing.

Line up these bells and play the same rhythm.

Play from left to right.

1.

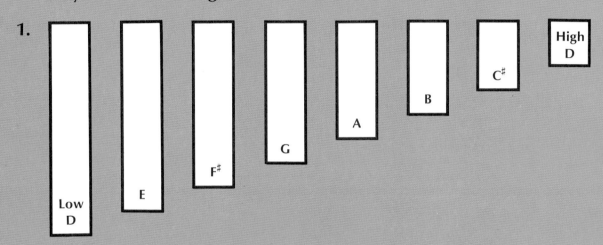

Now line up different bells and play the same rhythm.

2.

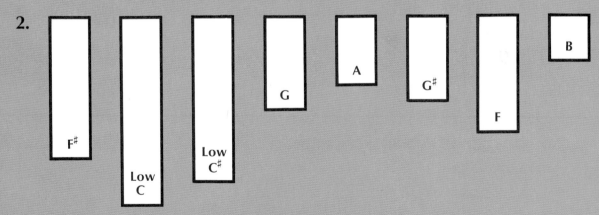

Which row has an important ending tone?

Which does not?

Which is tonal?   Which is atonal?

Match the drawings on page 167 with each row.

INDEX

POEMS

PICTURE CREDITS

3 4 5 6 7 8 9 10—RRD—85 84 83 82

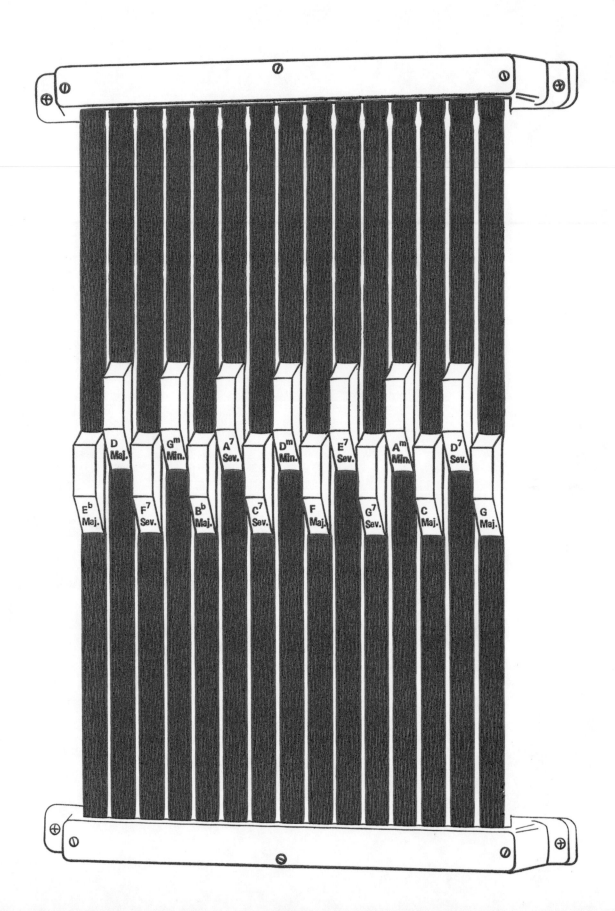